Open and Closed Economies

Roderick Macdonald

Open and Closed Economies

Lessons from the Philippines and Vietnam

palgrave
macmillan

Roderick Macdonald
International Business
UEH-ISB
Ho Chi Minh City, Vietnam

ISBN 978-3-030-79533-7 ISBN 978-3-030-79534-4 (eBook)
https://doi.org/10.1007/978-3-030-79534-4

This Palgrave Macmillan imprint is published by the registered company Springer Nature Switzerland AG
The registered company address is: Gewerbestrasse 11, 6330 Cham, Switzerland

Preface

My first recollection of the Philippines was a picture in the Montreal Gazette showing a number of men descending from a bus. They were participants in a Filipino Elvis look-alike contest. I was about ten years old at the time and I have since learned many things to love and respect about the Philippines, but this first impression remains: an Asiatic people heavily influenced by the United States of America and with no shame in having a good time.

My second recollection came when I was 20. It was the first time I came across large numbers of Filipinos. It was not in the Philippines, however. It was in Rome, Italy. I did not understand the reason until it was explained to me that many Filipinos had to leave their country to find well-paying jobs. This second impression of the Philippines still remains true today.

After that time, I began to meet and make Filipino friends, but my third major impression of the Philippines came when I was nearly 40, travelling to Rome from Barcelona. I opted out of a conference to circumnavigate the Vatican with a close friend. The conference was given by Cory Aquino, ex-president of the Philippines. I was told afterwards how she spoke through tears about the plight and suffering of large swathes of the Philippine population. Later I would learn more about the bloodless People Power Revolution that led to her coming to power. This strong impression of her personal compassion remains today, but I no longer see the People Revolution as a turning point in the history of her country.

My childhood passed more or less oblivious of the struggles between Vietnamese regimes, with the French colonisers and the American domino theorists. I was a young university professor walking the hallways when I overheard a girl speaking with a very open *joual* accent (a way of speaking French typical of the Québec countryside and some sections of Montréal). I turned and saw a very Asian face that belonged to a second-generation Vietnamese immigrant. By then I was learning how successfully the Vietnamese were integrating into Western societies after fleeing the new regime installed in 1975. I also had two close friend of Vietnamese origin—Charles, a finance professor who still finds the time to act as world grand master of Viet Vo Dao, and Quang, a manager at the International Civil Aviation Organisation. It was with Charles that I circumnavigated the Vatican.

Ho Chi Minh said that 'Americans are our enemies, but after the war they will be our friends'. This has certainly proven the case, at least in the attitude of the Vietnamese. Although the war museums in the country do not hesitate to present the American armed forces as the bad guys, the people in the street are definitely open-minded and welcoming, perhaps particularly in the South and centre of Vietnam. They are hard-working and pragmatic people focussed on improving the prosperity of their family and of their country.

Both countries are heart-throbs of economists and investors at the moment because of their rapid economic growth. However, as I began to visit both countries since 2010, I could not help but contrast the two nations. While it is true that the Philippines are wealthier than Vietnam as measured by GDP per capita, particularly in 2010 as the gap is narrowing, I could not help but feel that store prices were too high for most consumers. Even as a tourist, I saw a strong contrast in the price of low- to mid-range hotels, partly a reflection of real estate prices, partly a reflection of the nature of the demand in both countries. There were other differences as well. In Vietnam, most things worked. In the Philippines, many things were complicated. Misery was very visible in the Philippines, whereas I have never seen someone living on the street in Vietnam (although I did see poverty in the city and the countryside).

In 2018 I edited a book on the ASEAN Economic Community that included a chapter on each country. Both chapters were very upbeat, but I remained sceptical about the Philippine economy. How can you be satisfied when such a large portion of your population works abroad to gain a decent salary, often facing harrowing conditions of exploitation including physical violence and always separating families? It seemed to me that rapid increase in the GDP statistic was not telling the whole story.

When I began teaching international business to undergraduates at the International School of Business of UEH in Vietnam, I decided that my students need to appreciate how Vietnam had made its way out of poverty. I used the contrasting economic itineraries of Singapore and the Philippines in the second half of the twentieth century to highlight the contribution of foreign capital and trade as a precedent for Vietnam's policies. This in turn naturally led to the idea of this book that compares Vietnam and the Philippines.

There is limited discussion of corruption in this book, as unfortunately there is considerable corruption in both countries, so that the difference is insufficient to explain differing economic outcomes. The undue influence of interested parties upon economic policies in the Philippines does explain differing economic performance, but is not corruption. It is weak government.

Chapter 2 (as well as my 2020 publication about Vietnam) might give the impression that Vietnam is a paradise. I like Vietnam, but it is very imperfect, like everywhere else. The saying is that success in Ho Chi Minh is built upon business, while in Hanoi success comes from being close to power. I have met business people in the South who keep a low profile in the fear that too much business success will attract unwanted attention. Slums and squalor are not as visible as in the Philippines, but there are areas of great poverty and, in the cities at least, less pleasant surroundings.

Chapter 3 might give the impression that the wealthiest people in the Philippines are evil persons who do not care about their fellow citizens. That would be false. I have met rich and poor in the Philippines and they are like the rich and poor anywhere else. The problem of social injustice in the Philippines has arisen from leftovers of a bygone era reinforced by decades of various individuals pursuing their own personal benefit just one more time. Perhaps for that reason, it remains invisible to most people who are born and die there.

Finally, this book does not discuss two related topics: globalisation and offshore financial services. Globalisation tends to emphasise the political and standardising cultural and social consequences of increasing international trade, including trade in beauty products, fashion and media. The emphasis of this book is upon the economic benefits and drawbacks of increasing international trade. Offshore financial services are an important component (and facilitator) of international trade, but I have decided to exclude it for this book. Neither Vietnam nor the Philippines is currently a major player in financial services. Blockchain and other technical advances may change offshore finance more quickly and radically than additive manufacturing may change international merchandise trade. Excluding offshore financial services might seem odd in a book arguing for the international mobility of capital; however, I did not want to confound that mobility with the reduced regulation and tax evasion often associated with offshore finance.

George Ekins has reviewed the English and the logic of this book as an intelligent layperson. Any shortcomings are due to my obstinacy.

Ho Chi Minh City, Vietnam
March 2021

Roderick Macdonald

Contents

Notes on Contributors

Prosper Bernard is a professor of management at the University of Quebec in Montreal where he was previously vice-rector. Professor Bernard manages an M.B.A. in China. He has published numerous books and scientific papers on Asia and supervised many student dissertations on Asia.

Roderick Macdonald lectures in international business at the International School of Business of the University of Economics Ho Chi Minh City. He has published *Eurocritical* (2018), *Southeast Asia and the ASEAN Economic Community* (2019) and *The Economy and Business Environment of Vietnam* (2020) with Palgrave Macmillan since retiring from ESG-UQAM, Canada.

Trung Q. Nguyen is the Head of Department, Management, School of Business and Management, RMIT Vietnam. He is co-author of books on *Political Economy of Vietnam's Industrial Transformation* (Springer Nature, 2021) and on Business Forecasting (Lao Dong Publisher, 2016) as well as author or co-author of more than 25 academic articles, book chapters and conference papers since 2007.

Michel Plaisent is full professor in the department of Management, ESG-UQAM. He is coordinator of three MOU for research collaboration and supervises doctoral students from several Southeastern Asia universities. He presided the 10th International Conference on Education, Economics, Humanities and Social Sciences held at International School of Business, University of Economics Ho Chi Minh City.

List of Figures

List of Tables

CHAPTER 1

Open Economies, Closed Economies and a Case Study

Roderick Macdonald, Prosper Bernard, and Michel Plaisent

Abstract National leaders currently praise the advantages of free trade while simultaneously pursuing self-sufficiency and consumption of local produce. Theoretical and empirical economic research of the past 150 years returned mixed results regarding both free trade and foreign investment. This book uses a case study methodology to answer the question: can an economy open to trade and foreign direct investment increase the prosperity of the nation? The case study will contrast the economy of the Philippines from 1965 to 1994 with the economy of Vietnam from 1990 to 2014.

Keywords Autarkeia · Economic nationalism · Isolationism · Open economy · Closed economy · Free trade · Foreign direct investment · Quotas · Tariffs · Prosperity

R. Macdonald, *Open and Closed Economies*,
https://doi.org/10.1007/978-3-030-79534-4_1

Introduction

> We will: champion open economies… (Excerpt from G7 leaders' statement on February 19, 2021)

Any such statement is the result of a discussion among the leaders of the G7 countries, and is at once a commitment among the leaders, a message to their constituents and a message to the other nations of the world. How sincere they are and how faithful they will be to the statement may be open to debate, but what exactly is an open economy, and why would it be proposed as a good thing? An open economy is one that permits the free movement of goods and services, capital and labour across its borders—in other words, entering and leaving the nation. In practice, the free movement of labour is usually left aside except for some very exceptional cases such as the European Union.

This book will not deal extensively with the mobility of labour. Although this is an important issue, the data available tend to be heavily skewed towards political migration (fleeing persecution, for example) and irregular economic migration. A separate study and different skills would be required to investigate this question.

Although the openness of borders to the movement of capital is less discussed, politics and policies are factors that may dampen or facilitate both international trade and foreign investment. Recent years have seen the rise of populist politicians in many countries, and many proclaim economic nationalism as part of their political platforms. Even some supposedly non-populist politicians are doing so. The essence of economic nationalism is that a nation would be better off by limiting international trade as well as foreign ownership of business assets with the country's borders. Although this is contrary to the notions of liberal economics, it is also true that a nation could isolate itself while simultaneously allowing free rein to competition within its borders, intervening only to protect ownership, enforce contracts and do whatever else is necessary to enhance the freedom of the market where markets are appropriate (free markets in garbage disposal, education and health services—as we shall perhaps see with the management of the Covid-19 pandemic around the globe—do not seem to serve economies well). In any case, the discourse against international trade has increased, especially based on three arguments:

1. Foreign competition causes unemployment (rather than poor domestic policy—or poor implementation—for re-training and re-purposing the unemployed).
2. Domestic security precludes the participation of unreliable businesses in critical infrastructure (thus Taiwan's proximity to China and prominence in microprocessor fabrication would be a danger for the U.S.A.).
3. Much international trade is not truly free in any case, either because some nations manipulate their currency to keep their exports artificially cheap, or because some nations make access to their domestic markets conditional on ceding intellectual property.

The Covid-19 pandemic has strengthened the second argument as most nations had to import critical medical equipment. Although it is unrealistic to imagine most countries to be able to produce state-of-the-art medical equipment, the argument does hold sway in the United States of America.

In addition, some leaders—including some behind the G7 statement above—maintain an open economy discourse while enacting policies that at least partially close their national economies, or at least for some potential trading partners.

This debate between isolationism versus international trade may likely lead to regional trade blocs mostly decoupled from China, and perhaps one organised around China. This is mostly a political and media debate that partly confuses two issues: the issue of whether China is a desirable trading partner and the issue of whether it is desirable to have any trading partner. There is also some tendency to blend this debate into issues of geopolitical power and strategy.

The geopolitical and China issues will be put aside in this book. Instead, this book examines whether permitting the free movement of capital, goods and services across borders be good for the economy within those borders. There is a possible philosophical—ethical—response about the state respecting the rights and freedom of the individual, but this book will not enter into that area. This book only considers the pragmatic issue of whether an open economy is advantageous for prosperity of the nation. It proceeds using a case study about free trade and mobility of capital, the latter particularly in the form of foreign direct investment.

This case study approach differs from most of the work done on international trade and foreign direct investment as to methodology. It also differs in the question asked: can international trade and foreign direct investment be beneficial to the host nation? The questions about the causes of trade and investment and about the patterns of trade and investment targeted by most research carried out since David Ricardo's time are not addressed. These are separate questions, although not totally irrelevant to the question of universal advantage. For example, foreign direct investment is in great part motivated by profitability, and this may lead to a race to the bottom by host nations or regions competing for foreign investment, with ultimate advantage to the investor and perhaps the home nation, but not to the host nation. This and similar issues are excluded to focus solely on the possibility that international trade and foreign direct investment be beneficial to the host nation.

Of course, no country's government objects to the arrival of foreign capital, but it may limit access to foreign loans, and limit the degree of ownership available for foreign investment. If a foreign investor can provide 100% of funds for a project in a given country, but has no management control over the use of those funds, few foreigners will invest in that country. Most countries would be happy to allow businesses within their borders to export, as long as domestic markets are sufficiently served. However, it is difficult to export if you do not allow imports, and this unwanted competition for domestic businesses leads some governments to close down international trade. These realities are taken for granted in the question asked: Are international trade (including openness to imports) and foreign direct investment (with proportionate foreign ownership of the means of production) beneficial to the host nation?

The case study consists in a comparison of the historical experiences of two countries: Vietnam and the Philippines. Vietnam exemplifies a nation achieving increasing prosperity due to an economy open to trade and to capital. The Philippines exemplifies a nation mired in stagnation because its economy is closed to trade and to capital.

However, the contrast between the two economies is not that simple. Different time periods are involved. In addition, the openness and closedness of each economy is relative—neither is perfectly autarkic nor perfectly open to trade and capital.

Time period. The economies of both have been among the fastest growing in the world in the first two decades of this century. The comparison, however, is not between the two nations in the twenty-first century. The comparison is between the Philippines in the 35 years from 1960

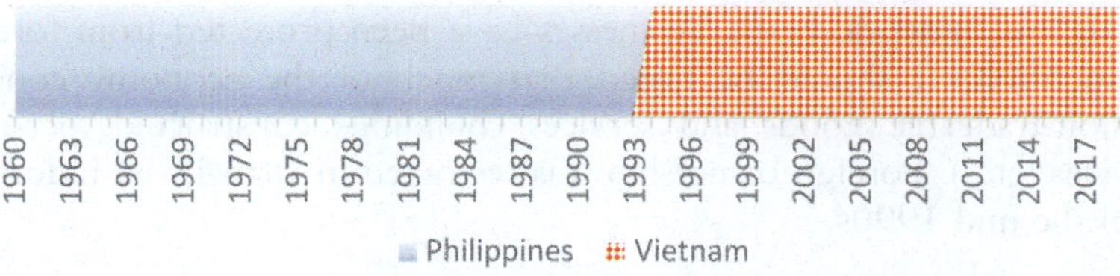

Fig. 1.1 Comparison years

until 1994 and Vietnam in the 25 years from the end of the US embargo on that country (1994–2018; since both the initial and final year are counted, that is 25 years of data) as presented in Fig. 1.1.

The World Bank provides data for the Philippines from 1960. Although the Penn World Table and the Maddison project each provide data for earlier dates, they are limited in scope. The Groningen Growth and Development Centre database provides useful data from 1950 that is also limited in scope, and excludes Vietnam. The starting date of 1960 also diminishes the impact of the Second World War and excludes a brief but catastrophic period of free trade between the Philippines and the United States of America. The Philippines, after this experience, closed the doors to imports and foreign ownership, and only partially opened the doors to the import of some goods not produced domestically in the subsequent decades. The country began to allow foreign ownership in some industries in the mid-1990s, with the effects becoming manifest thereafter.

In contrast, Vietnam has been relatively open to trade and foreign investment since 1994 until the present. This is somewhat of simplification, but serves to explain the time limits of the comparison.

GDP per capita increased about 40% in the Philippines during the chosen time period. The same statistic more than *tripled* in Vietnam—in fewer years. For precision's sake and perhaps beyond the margin of error in national accounting, 1.39 times over 35 years compared to 3.62 times in 25 years, using constant 2010 US dollars.

Relative openness. Although Vietnam has aggressively pursued openness to trade and capital, it remains a communist state and as such has a large number of state-owned enterprises protected from competition, be it domestic or foreign-owned. The Philippines, on the other hand, has allowed importation of some products and services since the

1960s, but most domestic businesses have been protected from foreign competition. It should be noted that much of the economy consists in non-tradeable goods and services (buildings constructed, personal services, etc.). Foreign ownership was restricted in virtually all industries until the mid-1990s.

In spite of this incomplete openness for both countries and the different time periods covered, the case study seems to provide a clear contrast in openness and consequent prosperity. There is no absolutely closed economy. The Philippines is as near to closed economy as can be found while excluding catastrophic extreme cases such as North Korea. And the Philippines performed poorly in the last half of the twentieth century. Vietnam, although a significant fraction of the economy is closed to any competition to state-owned enterprise, does provide an example of aggressive pursuit of a frontier open to trade and to capital. And Vietnam has been a top performer in terms of economic results.

Unfortunately, as soon as we widen the geographic scope just slightly, the differing results become less striking. Figure 1.2 shows that the Philippines underperformed by far compared to reference countries. However, although Vietnam outperformed most reference countries, it was slightly bested by the narrowest reference group of Asia Pacific countries members of the International Bank for Reconstruction and Development (IBRD) or the International Development Association (IDA). This somewhat superior performance poses a difficulty, because this difference is explained by the Asian Tigers: East Asian countries showing remarkable performance gains in the latter half of the twentieth century. We can add China to Hong Kong, Japan, Korea, Singapore and Taiwan (this last omitted in World Bank statistics). Among these countries, Japan, Korea and Taiwan did not pursue open economic policies, while China has pursued a mixed policy, protecting some private industries besides state-owned enterprises.

The Question

The question as to the link between openness to trade and capital on the one hand and prosperity on the other is not easily formulated in a way that permits a meaningful answer.

Adam Smith and David Ricardo provided insights as to how openness to trade can increase prosperity. Smith argued that international

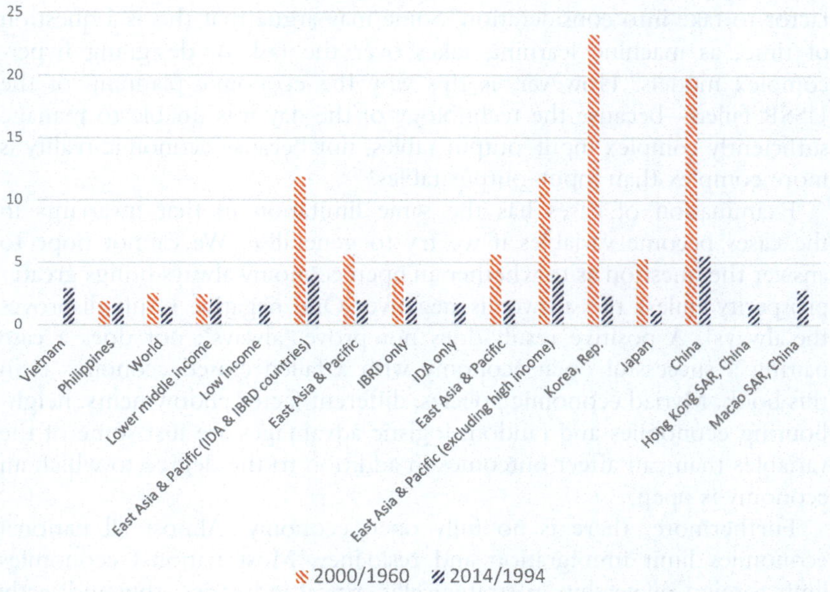

Fig. 1.2 GDP per capita change compared. The patterned columns represent the ratio of end year to start year values. IDA and IBRD countries: members of the International Bank for Reconstruction and Development and the International Development Association (*Source* Author's calculations based on World Bank national accounts data, and OECD National Accounts data files)

trade allows us to benefit from the strengths of our trading partners. Ricardo offered the argument that even an economy superior to all others across all industries still can benefit from trade if productivity varies across industries. These are insights, not mathematical or natural laws and not hypotheses to be tested. As economics became mathematised towards the end of the nineteenth century, their insights were translated into models that could be tested against reality (the empirical stream of literature) or refined either by varying additional assumptions (the mainstream theoretical literature) or sometimes by using modelling and simulations with more variables and assumptions than the human brain can comfortably manage. Both theoretical and empirical work, however, confront the fact that economies and national economic policies manifest more 'independent' variables than any model conceived. There is always one more factor to take into consideration. Some may argue that this is a question of time, as machine learning takes over the task of designing hyper-complex models. However, is this why the economic planning of the USSR failed—because the technology of the day was unable to manage sufficiently complex input–output tables, not because economic reality is more complex than input–output tables?

Examination of cases has the same limitation in that invariants in the cases become variables if we try to generalise. We cannot hope to answer the question as to whether an open economy always brings greater prosperity unless the answer is negative. One negative result disproves the'always'. A positive result does not prove 'always'; nor does a case pairing a successful open economy with a failed closed economy as in this book. Myriad economic policies, different factor endowments, neighbouring economies and random logistic advantages are just some of the variables than can affect outcomes in addition to the degree to which an economy is open.

Furthermore, there is no fully open economy. Almost all national economies limit immigration and residency. Most national economies limit foreign ownership in strategically critical industries, thus indirectly discouraging some avenues of foreign direct investment. Other movements of funds may also be limited to control narcotics and terror (albeit often half-heartedly). Food and health items are usually subject to sanitary or safety controls even if no trade barrier is intended.

Still, we can perhaps answer the question as to whether a more open economy *can* facilitate prosperity. This does not mean that closing the frontier to trade and foreign ownership, at least temporarily, might not also facilitate prosperity, as Chang (2003) and Shin and Chang (2003, noting particularly section 4.2) and Studwell (2013) have argued.

An open economy can offer a solution to the conundrum that poorer nations face in the pursuit of prosperity. Prosperity comes from productive human work. Human work is more productive when it is well-tooled and organised. Theoretically, a poor country could provide organisation (although logistics and meagre business experience in fact limit even organisation), but it cannot afford expensive tools and machinery. Foreign funding of machinery can resolve this problem. Since individual workers are more productive, there is room for them to earn higher wages, and thus afford purchasing a higher volume of produce. Access to foreign markets amplifies this effect. More affluent foreign clients can pay higher prices, increasing the currency measure of the national product. Human work is productive only if there are sufficiently solvent clients with the capacity of giving it high value. It would seem then that an economy open to foreign investment and open to trade is a solution. This includes importing. Imports can supply superior and/or cheaper materials, parts and design, all important for the international competitiveness of the exporting firms. Also, being able to export usually involves reciprocity with trade partners.

What Has Economics Research Taught Us About the Link Between Openness and Prosperity?

Research on Capital Mobility in the Form of Foreign Direct Investment

Economists would expect that foreign investment arriving in an economy would lead to growth by boosting the value produced by the workers in that economy. In addition to the immediate effect of multiplying the productivity of workers, foreign direct investment (FDI) can also involve the transfer both of technology (in the form of better machines and new processes and operator training) and management know-how.[1] This depends on the definition of FDI as distinct to indirect or portfolio foreign investment. Total ownership probably is linked to transfer of knowledge, a minority position less so, although even a 10% participation constitutes FDI (UNCTAD 2007) in most data sources.

The benefit of additional investment increasing productivity should always hold for all forms of FDI. Contrary to this expectation, not all empirical studies have found a positive relationship between FDI and economic growth, although most have.[2] Lasbrey et al. (2018) reviewed 35 empirical studies carried out between 1980 and 2018, of which 22 found a positive relation. Among the 13 that did not find a positive relation, 9 were limited in scope either in length of time, or in number of countries. Four studies did have a large data set: 88 countries from 1960 to 1992 (Bosworth and Collins 1999), 75 countries from 1938 to 1990 (Kentor 1998), 47 countries from 1970 to 2000 (Schneider 2005), 62 countries over 1975–2000 (Jyun 2008). There are many more empirical studies, but these 35 are representative of the range of results obtained: mostly a positive relation, but mixed results are frequent enough to raise questions.

The reason is that numerous other factors influence economic performance. For example, if foreign direct investment does not lead to increased gross capital formation because domestic investors withdraw, then there will be little or no change in economic performance. Pervasive poor-quality projects—perhaps because of systematic fraud—would also dilute any effect of foreign direct investment. Quality of institutions, preparedness of human capital, logistics and many other factors affect the FDI-prosperity relationship. Although some of these factors affect investment performance and thus should be linked to decreased FDI, in practice they remain a source of noise in detecting the relation between foreign investment and economic growth.

International Trade Theory and Empirical Work

Since the mid-nineteenth century, as economics drifted towards quantitative analysis, the theory of international trade has focussed on the patterns and causes of trade. The Heckscher–Ohlin approach before World War II as well as the more recent work of Bhagwati and many others involves mathematical modelling and thus requires (or perhaps renders explicit) multiple assumptions that often do not hold in reality.[3] Scientific progress revolved around the loosening or variation of assumptions and has led to ever more complex models and sophisticated analyses without arriving at the holy grail of prediction.

The 'new' trade theory of the last two decades of the twentieth century attempts to explain the non-random structure of international trade after recalling that businesses engage in trading, not nations nor governments. Just as the industrial organisation school of economics begins with the observation that a significant portion of national economies are structured (not a random distribution of an infinite number of buyers and sellers of identical products), the new trade theory observes than there are businesses that dominate significant portions of international trade, and seeks explanations. Although new trade theory did not primarily address the question of whether free trade is beneficial to the host nation, both the original observation and the explanations (increasing returns and scale, for example) have implications for the benefits vs drawbacks of free international trade: under conditions of universal free trade, some industries will be dominated by a small number of firms, and these may well be located in a smaller number of countries. Contrary to the inclination of most economists publishing in this stream of literature, this could be construed into an argument for economic nationalism to defend against foreign domination.

Trade and Growth

There are also abundant streams of literature on economic growth and on economic development and, within these, examination of the impact of trade. However, problems arise similar to those in the 'FDI and growth' stream. Straightforward efforts to correlate growth to trade meet with mixed results (see the lack of evident correlation, for example, in Fig. 1.3). This led to two developments: in methodology and in theory. Methodological developments involved recourse to different mathematical tools to analyse the data, in part to discount the effect of myriad other variables that affect growth. 'Ceteris paribus' posed a serious problem. Theoretical developments involved questioning the very meaning of prosperity and openness to trade. What does openness to trade mean? Is it a characteristic of the policy and laws that regulate trade? Or is it rather an observable fact: a high volume of trade, Higher exports/GDP, Higher trade/GDP or Higher imports/GDP? Should we take into account distance or logistic factors that make trade between countries more costly? Again, what does prosperity mean? Even if we exclude issue like environmental effects, the distribution of wealth and other developmental considerations, prosperity can be problematic to measure. Should we use gross domestic product (GDP) or gross national income (GNI) per capita? Should we first correct our statistics by taking purchasing power parity into account? Or should we eschew prosperity as the dependent variable and look at productivity of labour?

These questions would have lesser importance had the simple correlation of trade and wealth not failed, and they will inform the case study of the following chapters, that will examine both de facto and de iure indicators of openness to trade as well as various indicators of prosperity.

Empirical and Theoretical Work on Economic Openness

Efforts to link either trade or financial openness to growth and prosperity have led to a debate as to what precisely constitutes economic openness. The rise of web sites proposing indices of economic data has spread to this area, and several authors and organisations propose indices of economic openness or 'globalisation'. These indices measure different things and in fact have different purposes in spite of similarities.

For example, the Legatum Institute compiles an index of economic openness under the direction of Dr. Stephen Brien. This index tries to capture freedom of markets from government manipulation more than

Fig. 1.3 GDP per capita growth versus imports. The vertical axis measures ratio GDP per capita 2017 over GDP per capita in 1970 in current US dollars. The ratio is *not* a percentage. The current US dollar was used as a unit because constant currency unit statistics are not available for all countries and all years. The horizontal axis measures average imports as a percentage of GDP (***Data source*** World Bank national accounts data, and OECD National Accounts data files)

openness to foreign trade, capital and labour, as can be seen from its methodology disclosure (Legatum Institute 2020). The index fails to capture the manipulation of the Philippine economy by non-government interests, and Vietnam scores lower than the Philippines (= more manipulation in the opinion of Legatum), as might be expected for a communist regime. Although the index has its use, it is ineffective in contrasting how the economies of Vietnam and the Philippines welcome world trade and finance. It will not be used for the present case.

The KOF Swiss Economic Institute (Konjunkturforschungsstelle) publishes a globalisation index, and includes economic sub-indices.

One of the strengths of the case described in this book is the contrast between the Philippines and Vietnam. However, the KOF globalisation index for economic openness does not point to a strong contrast between the two countries. While this might be superficially explained by pointing out that the KOF index has been calculated since 1970 only, and so omits important years of economic nationalism in the Philippines, there is some other additional problem. We would expect the Philippines to be mostly closed and Vietnam mostly open today, but although the index ranks the Philippines in the bottom half at 104th place out of 203 countries, Vietnam obtains little difference in ranking at 95th place. The de jure rankings are even closer and reversed, with the Philippines placing 97th and Vietnam, 100th. Intuitively we think of de iure openness when we ask if a country is open to international trade, although the impact of this openness must be achieved through de facto trade. It also seems unlikely that Vietnam has a higher openness score than the Philippines from 1970 to 1994, years of war and then embargo imposed by the United States of America, particularly since the Marcos regime in the Philippines was seeking funding from abroad.

The reason the KOF index reveals far less contrast between the two economies might be diversity of trading partners, but hard data show this is not the case.

The KOF index estimates 'trade globalisation de facto' by combining trade (measured by imports and exports) normalised by GDP, with diversity of trading partners (roughly the number of different national destinations of exports and sources of imports). A 2006 paper by Kim and Park (2006) showed that the correlation of trade and growth becomes far stronger when diversity of trade partners is taken into account. Arguably, then, the diversity of trading partners is a dimension of openness. For that matter, diversity of exports and imports would also be dimensions of openness; the Observatory of Economic Complexity has the link between prosperity and diversity of merchandise exports (and, very recently, services) as its premise.

Figure 1.4 Concentration of trade partners presents the concentration—the non-dispersion—of trading partners. The metadata of the world bank statistic states that a 'country with trade (export or import) that is concentrated in a very few markets will have an index value close to 1. Similarly, a country with a perfectly diversified trade portfolio will have an index close to zero' (World Bank 2020). Vietnam has a lower score than the Philippines, and indeed approaches the score of Singapore, a country with extremely diversified trading partners. Diversity of trading partners should increase the contrast between Vietnam and the Philippines, not diminish it. Given the data on trade partner dispersal, as well as exports and import data, relatively similar KOF (economic) globalisation scores do not seem to be appropriate indicators for openness in the case comparing the Philippines and Vietnam and will not be used.

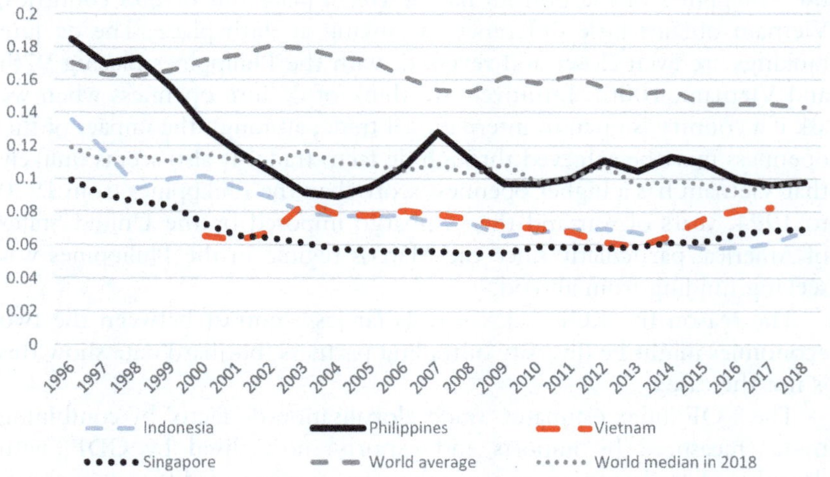

Fig. 1.4 Concentration of trade partners. Individual points are the Hirschman Herfindahl Market concentration index for the given country and year. Higher values indicate fewer trading markets, lower values indicate greater dispersion of trading partners (*Data source* The World Integrated Trade Solution [WITS])

In any case, this book takes a simpler approach. The contrast between the two cases is based upon the observed difference in levels of international trade and international financing in the two countries, de facto and de iure.

Gräbner et al. (2020) provides a general overview of efforts to measure economic openness, covering about 50 variables from 18 different sources. The results reinforce the impressions from the literature streams on trade and growth and on FDI and growth: changing the indicator of openness impacts the relation between openness and prosperity as much as changing the indicator of trade, FDI, or indeed the choice of starting and ending years of measurement. This does not necessarily mean such research is pointless, but it does reinforce the utility of examining specific cases.

The Evolution of the Volume of Foreign Direct Investment and of International Trade

Business investment in multiple countries has increased, as measured by foreign direct investment inflow in current US dollars and as a percentage of world GDP. However, this trend is far more sensitive to the economic and financial context than is GDP. The curve skyrocketed upwards in the years preceding the global financial crisis and then plummeted. It also fluttered with the telecom and dot.com busts of the turn of the century and dropped with the onset of the US–China trade war. See Fig. 1.5 World FDI inflows in current US dollars and Fig. 1.6 FDI net inflows as a percentage of GDP.

World exports of both goods and services (in current US dollars) have also increased for 55 years from 1960, with a momentary hesitation from 2000 to 2001 (see Fig. 1.7 World exports and Fig. 1.8 World exports as a percentage of GDP). It then dropped in 2015 and 2016, increased to 19.6 trillion by 2018, then began to drop again. Thus, the statistic for world exports has decreased in value several times since 2014. This downward drift predates the US–China trade war initiated by the Donald Trump administration.

However, this should not be interpreted as a trend to decreasing international trade anterior to that trade war. The statistic has decreased in value primarily because of decrease in the price of crude petroleum. This price affects trade volume through at least three channels. The price of petroleum impacts the cost of transport, and thus the dispersion of trade

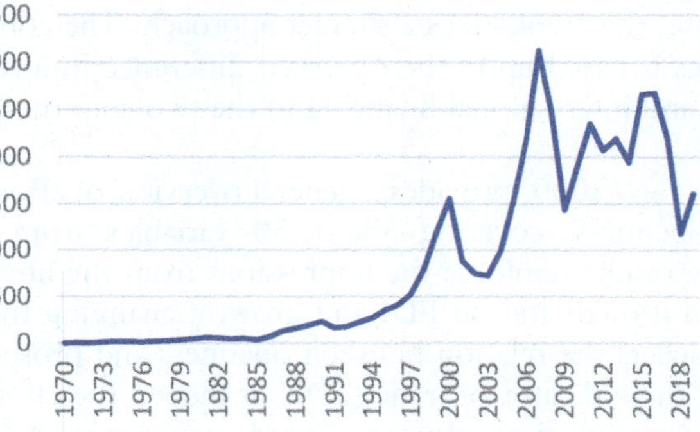

Fig. 1.5 World FDI inflows in current US dollars (*Data sources* International Monetary Fund, Balance of Payments database, supplemented by data from the United Nations Conference on Trade and Development and official national sources)

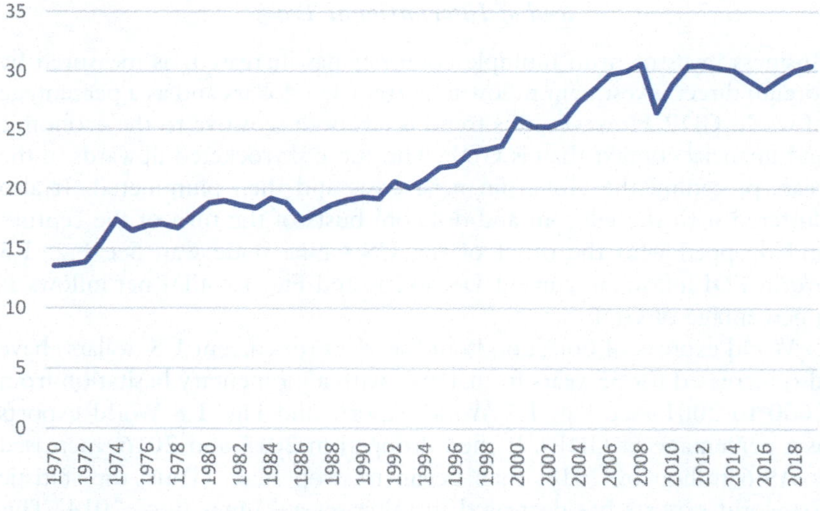

Fig. 1.6 FDI net inflows as a percentage of GDP (*Data sources* World Bank national accounts data, and OECD National Accounts data files)

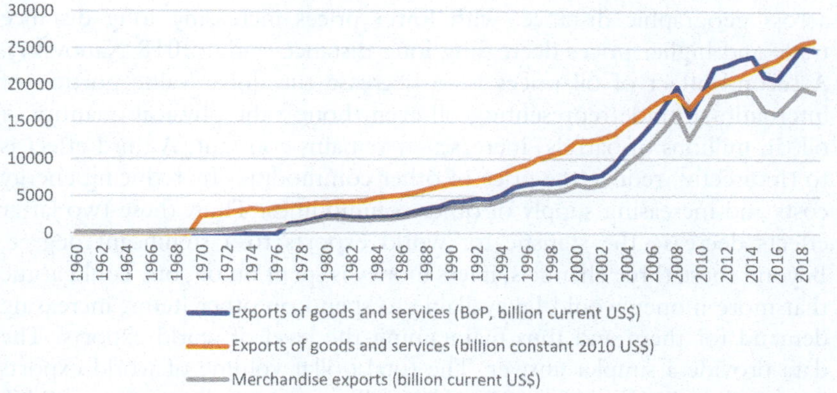

Fig. 1.7 World exports (*Data sources* World Bank national accounts data, and OECD National Accounts data files, International Monetary Fund, Balance of Payments Statistics Yearbook and data files, World Trade Organisation)

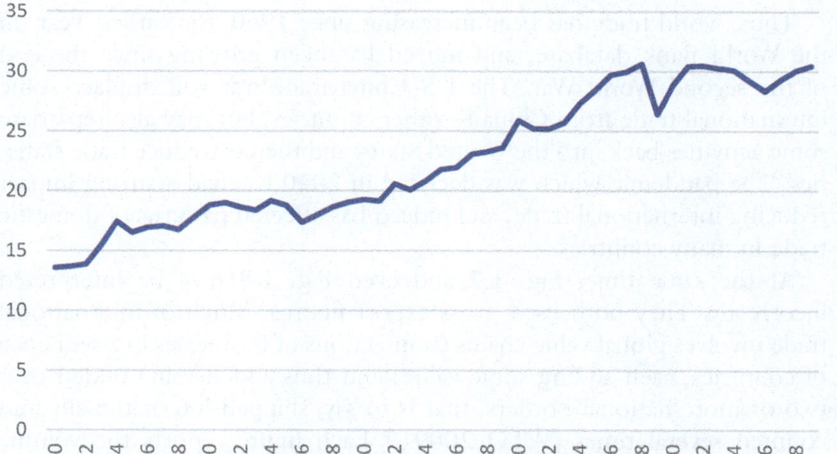

Fig. 1.8 World exports as a percentage of GDP (*Data sources* World Bank national accounts data, and OECD National Accounts data files)

across geographic distance, with lower prices increasing long distance trade and higher prices decreasing long distance trade (2018 Nanovsky). A second effect of oil prices is to decrease the dollar value portion of international trade representing oil even though the physical quantity of oil (in millions of barrels) increases or remains constant. A third effect is to (indirectly) reduce the price of other commodities by reducing energy costs and increasing supply of other commodities. Thus, these two latter effects decrease the statistic for world exports to a significant degree. Beyond these three channels, if less money is spent on oil, one could argue that more money would be available to spend on other items, increasing demand for them and thus maintaining the level of world exports. The data provide a simpler answer. The total dollar volume of world exports increased during both the 1970s (302 billion to 1.6 trillion in current US dollars) and the 2000–2014 (6.5 trillion current US dollars in 2000, 16.3 in 2008, 19.1 in 2014), both periods of increasing oil prices. The drop in world exports from 2014 to 2016 coincides with a decreasing price of oil.

Thus, world trade has been increasing since 1960, the earliest year on the World Bank database, and indeed has been growing since the end of the second World War. The US–China trade war will displace some international trade from China to other countries, but may also repatriate some activities back into the United States and thereby reduce trade statistics. The pandemic which was declared in 2020 has had a strong impact reducing international trade, and indeed has affected patterns of domestic trade in many countries.

At the same time, Fig. 1.7 and even Fig. 1.8 may be interpreted incorrectly. They both used gross export figures. Much of international trade involves global value chains (transactions of businesses in a sequence of countries, each adding some value) and thus added value traded over two or more national borders, that is to say, shipped internationally and counted several times (WTO 2009).[4] Each figure reports the volume of international shipments, not the amount of value added shipped. Table 1.1 illustrates the difference. Figure 1.9 presents world domestic value added shipped internationally as a percentage of world GDP. The percentages and especially the growth rate are far lower than in Fig. 1.8. This does not contradict the observed change in the nature of trade, nor does it mean that the reported figures are false. It does lead us to revisit the relation between trade and the generation of value added.

Table 1.1 Global value chains and national accounting

Country	*Import*	*Value added*	*Export*	*Accumulated Exports*
1	0	10	10	10
2	10	10	20	30
3	20	10	40	70
4	40	10	50	120
5	50	10	60	180
6	60	10	70	250

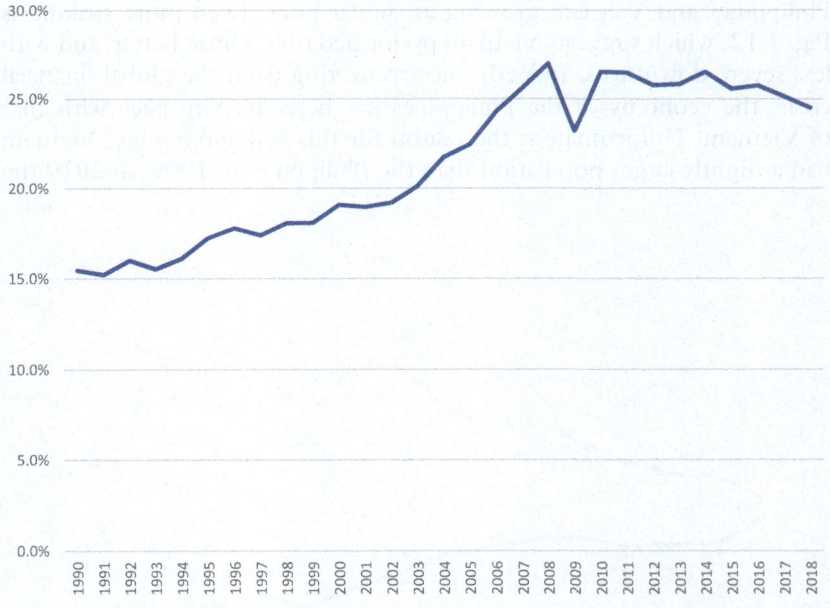

Fig. 1.9 Total domestic value added shipped internationally as a percentage of world GDP. Total domestic value added is the sum of direct and indirect domestic value. Using the Eora labels for statistics, VA_exp = DVA + DVX (*Data source* Author's calculations from EORA database, World Bank national accounts data, and OECD National Accounts data files)

Problems with the Philippines and Vietnam Case

Recent economic performance by the two countries provides a second problem. Both the Philippines and Vietnam have enjoyed rapid economic growth in the first two decades of the twenty-first century. Perhaps this seems to contradict any pro-trade and FDI message from the case. This is all the more so because the Philippines' openness to trade and FDI seemed to have faltered after initially opening up in the early 90s. The Fig. 1.10 shows that Vietnam is ever more open to trade, and the Philippines ever more closed. Surprising, Fig. 1.11 seems to show the Philippines and Vietnam growing at similar rates. Even more striking is Fig. 1.12, which suggests Vietnam performed only a little better, and with less severe downturns. Indeed, since recovering from the global financial crisis, the economy of the Philippines has been keeping pace with that of Vietnam. Unfortunately, the reason for this is demographic: Vietnam had a slightly larger population than the Philippines in 1999; in 2019 the

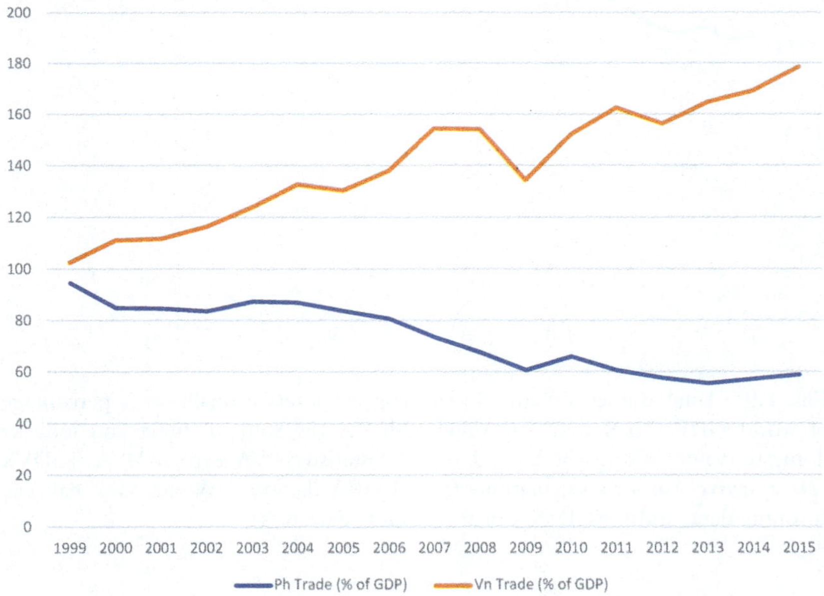

Fig. 1.10 Evolution of trade compared 1999–2015 (*Data Sources* World Bank national accounts data, and OECD National Accounts data files)

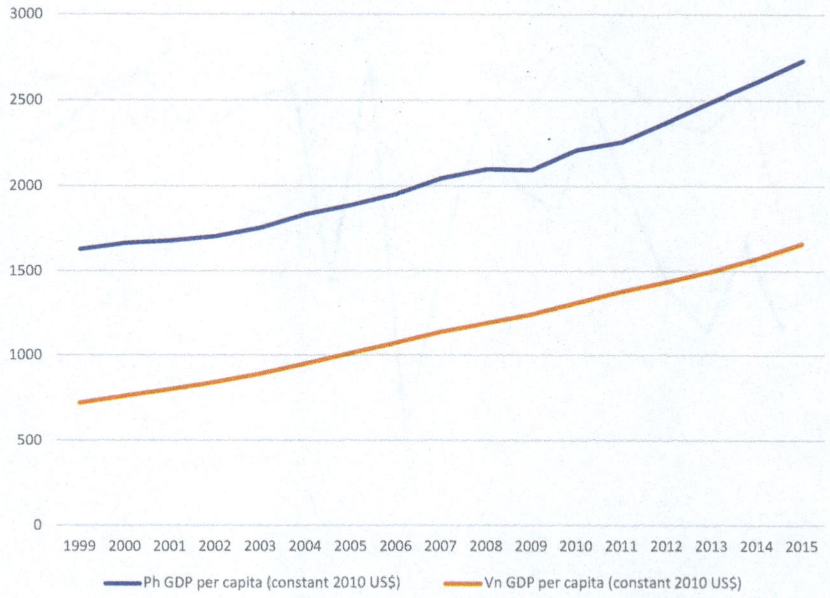

Fig. 1.11 Evolution of GDP per capita 1999–2019 (*Data sources* World Bank national accounts data, and OECD National Accounts data files)

Philippines was 10% larger. When arithmetic replaces visual inspection, the similarities disappear. Comparison CAGR prosperity indices (such as GDP per capita) for 1999–2019 shows that the economy of Vietnam clearly has outperformed that of the Philippines in the four most common prosperity indicators. Conceivably the best performing years for the Philippines were 2009–2014. Figure 1.13 shows the Philippines only approaches Vietnam in GDP per capita expressed in current international purchasing power parity dollars. As a consequence, recent impressive growth in the economy of the Philippines does not destroy the power of the case in this book. Chapter 4 will nonetheless return to this issue using the more detailed data of Chapters 2 (about the economy of Vietnam) and 3 (about the economy of the Philippines).

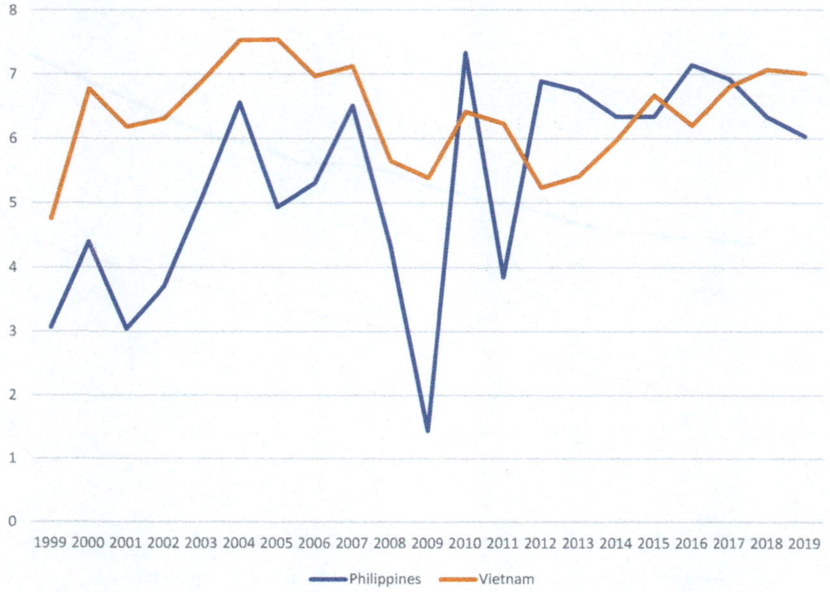

Fig. 1.12 GDP growth rates compared (*Data sources* World Bank national accounts data, and OECD National Accounts data files)

Fig. 1.13 CAGR of various prosperity indices over 2009–2014 for Philippines and Vietnam (*Data sources* Authors' calculations based on World Bank national accounts data, OECD National Accounts data files, the International Comparison Program of the World Bank, the World Development Indicators database, and the Eurostat-OECD PPP Programme)

Notes

1. There are exceptions, as some foreign investment projects may reserve proprietary knowledge technical work and upper management positions to home country employees.
2. Lejarraga and Ragoussis (2018) are far more confident that virtually all research shows FDI as positively impacting prosperity. See their Table 2. This stands in stark contrast with Alfaro and Charlton (2013).
3. There are abundant retrospectives of international trade theory such as De Feis (2016), Ethier (2013), Helpman (2006), Leamer and Levinsohn (1994), Mathur et al. (2017), Ruffin (2013), and Sen (2010). Regarding the difficulty in arriving at prediction, Bowen's (1989) review of Feneestra's Empirical Methods for International Trade mentions that 'Certainly, the 1960s and 1970s witnessed an explosion of research which found new patterns and puzzles and suggested that other causes of trade beside factor endowments were important. Of course using the standard model one could demonstrate other factors could cause trade, but the theoretical statements were difficult to translate into empirically testable hypothesis. Consequently, tests of trade theory locked with specified alternative hypotheses and the findings of such tests only serve to heightened frustration, not relieve it'.
4. Other consequences of this 'double counting' (Koopman 2012) are the volatility of trade statistics following any shock (OECD 2002) and danger of exaggerating the importance of imports from any given country and resulting trade imbalances as illustrated by the classic example of the import of iPhones from China into the U.S. (Xing and Detert 2010). This problem is partly addressed by the notion of trade in value added, for example, the OECD TIVA database.

References

Alfaro, Laura, and Andrew Charlton. 2013. Growth and the Quality of Foreign Direct Investment. In *The Industrial Policy Revolution. The Role of Government Beyond Ideology*, ed. Joseph E. Stiglitz and Justin Lin Yifu. Basingstoke: Palgrave Macmillan.

Bosworth, B.P., and Collins S.M. 1999. Capital Flows to Developing Economies: Implications for Savings and Investment. *Brookings Papers on Economics* 6: 145–165.

Bowen, Harry P. 1989. [Review of] Empirical Methods for International Trade. *Journal of International Economics* 27 (1–2): 191–196.

Chang, Ha-Joon. 2003. Kicking Away the Ladder: The "Real" History of Free Trade. Foreign Policy in Focus, December 30.

De Feis, George, and Grunewald, Donald, and De Feis, George. 2016. An International Trade Theory for Our Time: Trade Theory of Hyper-Globalization and Hyper-Information Flow, January 31. Available at SSRN https://ssrn.com/abstract=2725334 or http://dx.doi.org/10.2139/ssrn.2725334.

Ethier, Wilfred J. 2013. The Floating World: Issues in International Trade Theory, September 20. PIER Working Paper No. 13-052. Available at SSRN https://ssrn.com/abstract=2329780 or http://dx.doi.org/10.2139/ssrn.2329780.

Gräbner, C., Heimberger, P., Kapeller, J., and Springholz, F. 2020. Understanding Economic Openness: A Review of Existing Measures. *Review of World Economics* 157: 87–120.

Helpman, Elhanan, Trade, FDI, and the Organization of Firms. 2006. Harvard Institute of Economic Research Discussion Paper No. 2118, May. Available at SSRN https://ssrn.com/abstract=901426 or http://dx.doi.org/10.2139/ssrn.901426.

Jyun, Y.C. 2008. Does Foreign Direct Investment Promote Economic Growth: Evidence from Threshold Regression Analysis? *Economic Bulletin* 15 (12): 1–10.

Kentor, Jeffrey. 1998. The Long-Term Effects of Foreign Investment Dependence on Economic Growth, 1940–1990. *American Journal of Sociology* 103 (4) (January): 1024–1046.

Kim, Taegi, and Kuseung Park. 20062. 무역의 다양성과 교역상대국이 자국의 경제성장에 미친 영향 (The Impact of Trade Diversity and Trading Partners on Domestic Economic Growth). *East Asian Economic Review* 10 (1) (June): 29–56. Available at SSRN https://ssrn.com/abstract=3078401 or http://dx.doi.org/10.2139/ssrn.3078401.

Lasbrey, Anochiwa, Michael Enyoghasim, Agbanike Tobechi, Nkechi Uwajumogu, Basil Chukwu, and Ololo Kennedy. 2018. Foreign Direct Investment and Economic Growth: Literature from 1980 to 2018. *International Journal of Economics and Financial Issues* 8 (5).

Leamer, Edward E., and James A. Levinsohn. 1994. International Trade Theory: The Evidence, November. NBER Working Paper No. w4940. Available at SSRN https://ssrn.com/abstract=226540.

Legatum Institute. 2020. The Global Index of Economic Openness 2019. Methodology Report. Available at https://li.com/wp-content/uploads/2019/05/Country-and-Pillar-Profiles.pdf. Accessed November 21, 2020.

Lejárraga, Iza, and Alexandros Ragoussis. 2018. Beyond Capital. Monitoring Development Outcomes of Multinational Enterprise. International Finance Corporation (World Bank Group). Available at http://documents1.worldbank.org/curated/en/342571545336579695/pdf/WPS8686.pdf. Accessed December 12, 2020.

Mathur, Somesh K., Rahul Arora, Sarbjit Singh, and Amrita Roy. 2017. Developments in International Trade Theory and Gravity Modelling. In *Theorizing International Trade. An Indian Perspective*, ed. Somesh K. Mathur, Rahul Arora, and Sarbjit Singh. Basingstoke: Palgrave Macmillan.

Ruffin, Roy J. 2013. The Development of International Trade Theory. In *Palgrave Handbook of International Trade*, ed. D. Greenaway, R. Falvey, U. Kreickemeier, and D. Bernhofen, 15–38.

Schneider, P.H. 2005. International Trade, Economic Growth and Intellectual Property Rights: A Panel Data Study of Developed and Developing Countries. *Journal of Development Economics* 78 (2): 529–547.

Sen, Sunanda. 2010. International Trade Theory and Policy: A Review of the Literature, November 23. Levy Economics Institute Working Papers Series No. 635. Available at SSRN https://ssrn.com/abstract=1713843 or http://dx.doi.org/10.2139/ssrn.1713843.

Shin, Jang-Sup, and Ha-Joon Chang. 2003. *Restructuring 'Korea Inc.': Financial Crisis, Corporate Reform, and Institutional Transition*. London: Taylor & Francis Group

Studwell, Joe. 2013. *How Asia Works: Success and Failure in The World's Most Dynamic Region*. Grove Press.

UNCTAD. 2007. World Investment Report. Available at https://unctad.org/system/files/official-document/wir2007p4_en.pdf. Accessed November 12, 2020.

World Bank. 2020. Metadata for HH (Hirschman Herfindahl) Market Concentration Index. Available at https://tcdata360.worldbank.org/indicators/hh.mkt?country=PHL&indicator=2370&countries=VNM,SGP&viz=line_chart&years=1988,2015. Accessed November 21, 2020.

WTO. 2009. International Trade Statistics 2009. World Trade Organization WTO Publications. Available at http://www.wto.org/english/res_e/statis_e/its2009_e/its09_toc_e.htm. Accessed November 4, 2021.

Xing, Yuqing, and Neal Detert. 2010. How the iPhone Widens the United States Trade Deficit with the People's Republic of China. ADBI Working Paper Series No 257. Asian Development Bank Institute. http://www.adbi.org/workingpaper/2010/12/14/4236.iphone.widens.us.trade.deficit.prc/. Accessed November 5, 2021.

CHAPTER 2

Vietnam: Open, Growing, but with so Much More Potential

Roderick Macdonald and Trung Q. Nguyen

Abstract Previous to 1994, Vietnam was either a colony of France, at war or under a US-led embargo. Since that time, it has opened up its economy to trade and foreign direct investment. The result was a massive increase in trade, and, through trade, the prosperity of the country. The chapter ends with suggestions to extend and improve this performance.

Keywords Free trade · FDI · Foreign direct investment · Vietnam · Prosperity · Open economy

Vietnam in Earlier Centuries

Europeans arrived in Vietnam in the sixteenth century (some Chinese texts suggest the Romans had been there much earlier), but little of lasting political consequence happened until the French became involved in rise of the Nguyen dynasty at the start of the nineteenth century. The French became militarily active in the late 1850s, bringing the full country (as well as present-day Laos and Cambodia) under its dominion by 1883.

R. Macdonald, *Open and Closed Economies*,
https://doi.org/10.1007/978-3-030-79534-4_2

In its thrust to exploit the peninsula, France introduced rubber plantations and developed rice. The coloniser also developed the infrastructure, notably building a North–South railroad that helped unite a country historically fragmented from South to North, as well as extending the road and bridge network and improving ports. It also contributed to the development of human capital in three ways. Western medicines improved the health of Vietnamese, particularly in the early twentieth century. More advanced education, including the sciences and engineering, became more widely available. Finally, the French introduced plantations, leading to a large land-owning class and the existence of indigenous capitalists. The presence of the French was more strongly felt around Hanoi, and these beneficial effects had a greater impact in the North.

In spite of these contributions, the administration of the colony was not very effective except in the imposition of French decisions over local interests. There were as many French administrators in Vietnam as British administrators in all of British India (which extended to modern day Pakistan and Bangladesh, each as populous as Vietnam).

One French-educated Vietnamese, Nguyen Sinh Cung, adopted a series of pseudonyms throughout his career. He lived in the United States of America (1912 and 1913), Britain (intermittently between 1913 and 1919), France (1919 to 1923, becoming interested in left wing politics), Russia (1923 to 1924), China (1924–1927) followed by a flurry of travel through Russia, France and other European countries, and then Thailand, India and Shang'hai (1927–1929). In Hong Kong he united two political groups into the Communist party of Vietnam, was arrested and then released (1929–1933). He returned to Russia for further 'education' (1933–1938) before serving as advisor to Communist military forces in China (1938–1941). He then returned to Vietnam to undertake his great life's work: under the name Ho Chi Minh he repulsed the French and then the Americans to re-unite Vietnam in 1975. He died in 1969, after refusing to make concessions to Richard Nixon to end the war with America and the Southern regime.

At the end of its war in Vietnam, the United States policed an embargo upon trade with Vietnam that was maintained until 1994. During these nearly 20 embargo years following the war, the government of Vietnam first experimented with doctrinaire communist economic policies with the aid of Soviet funding (Hoan 1991) that would disappear with the Soviet empire, and then began to settle upon a 'socialist-oriented' free market in the mid-1980s.

The result was that any economic contribution of French colonisation could not benefit Vietnam until the last few years of the twentieth century.

Recent Economic Performance

Since the mid-1990s, however, Vietnam has seen steady economic growth. GDP has more than quadrupled since 1996, and GDP per capita has more than tripled (see Figs. 2.1 and 2.2). In these ratios it has outperformed the two reference countries of Indonesia and the Philippines in both figures. It has also outperformed Singapore for that period. Like the

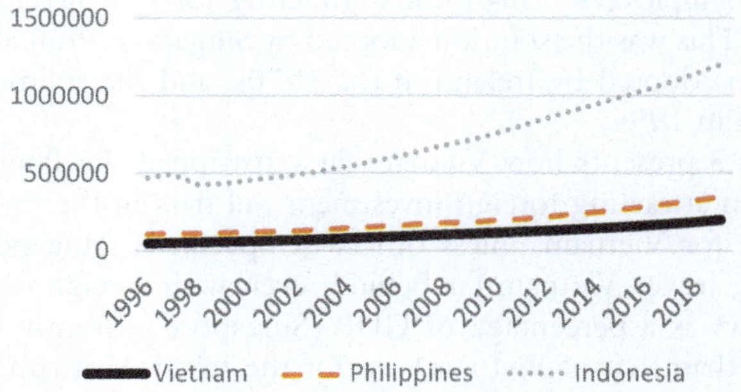

Fig. 2.1 GDP constant 2010 US dollars (*Data source* World Bank national accounts data, and OECD National Accounts data files)

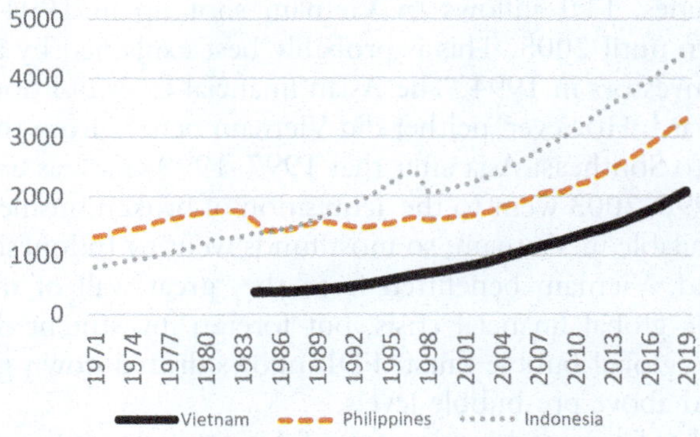

Fig. 2.2 GDP per capita (*Data source* World Bank national accounts data, and OECD National Accounts data files)

Philippines, Vietnam has been among the top large countries for consistent fast growth over the past years (as calculated by comparing GDP growth for all countries on the World Bank database, then excluding countries with small populations).

A wealthy country is one in which production by the population is highly valued by solvent buyers. Such production implies having machinery and acquiring the skills—difficult when you are poor. The requirement of solvent customers is also difficult when a country is poor. The solution is to use machinery purchased by businesses from wealthy countries to sell to buyers in wealthier countries, and to learn skills from the owners and managers of foreign businesses as well as from their senior operational employees. This means attracting foreign direct investment for export. This was the solution adopted by Singapore from about 1970, the solution adopted by Ireland in the 1970s, and the solution adopted by Vietnam in 1994.

Figure 2.3 presents how Vietnam far outstripped the Philippines and Indonesia in attracting foreign investment (all data in the figures of this chapter are for Vietnam unless otherwise specified). Singapore, on the other hand, leaves Vietnam far behind, even with foreign direct investment inflows as a percentage of GDP (Singapore currently has a GDP 40% larger than that of Vietnam). As for the trend, Vietnam and Singapore reacted to external financial shocks in different ways. The Asian financial crisis of 1997–1998, the 2000–2001 telecom and dotcom busts, and the 2007–2010 global financial and economic crises all led to catastrophic drops of FDI inflow into Singapore that were followed by equally rapid recoveries. FDI inflows to Vietnam shot up in 1994, and then tended down until 2005. This is probably best explained by a first wave of pioneer investors in 1994. The Asian financial crisis did not affect this drift downward. However, neither did Vietnam benefit from the return of investment to Southeast Asia after that 1997–1998 crisis, as early moneys from late 1998–2003 went to the acquisition of broken businesses. These were not available in Vietnam, so most funds went to Indonesia, Malaysia and Thailand. Vietnam benefitted from the 'great wall of money' that preceded the global financial crisis, but foreign investment did not dry up when the global bubble burst; FDI inflows drifted down gradually to about a third above pre-bubble levels.

Vietnam has been moderately successful in attracting inflows of foreign capital. If we exclude countries with a population under 10 million, Vietnam is among the top ten in the world in accumulating foreign direct

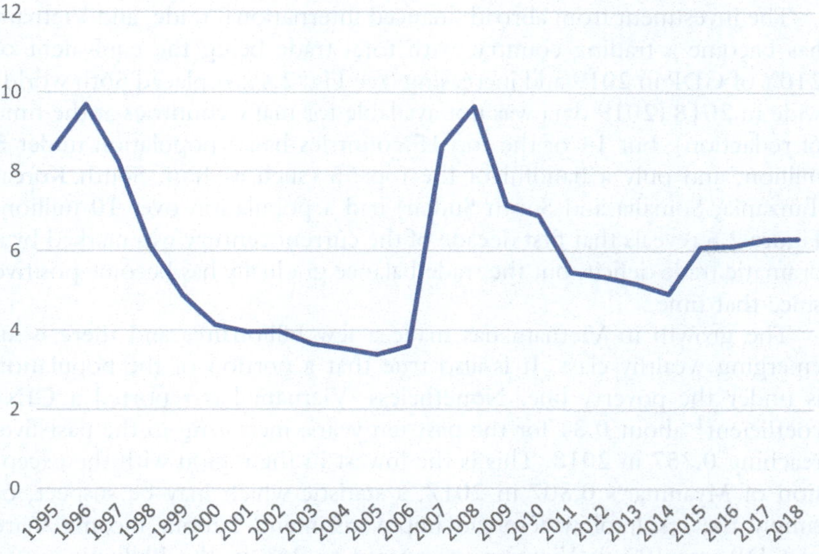

Fig. 2.3 Foreign direct investment as a percentage of *GDP* (*Data sources* International Monetary Fund, International Financial Statistics and Balance of Payments databases, World Bank, International Debt Statistics, and World Bank and OECD GDP estimates)

investment (measured as a fraction of GDP). If we exclude countries with populations under 20 million, only Mozambique has done better than Vietnam. Smaller populations correlate with a smaller agriculture, forestry and fisheries sector and limited infrastructure shortcomings, and thus promise higher average return on investment. When we compare growth in GDP per capita for Mozambique and Vietnam, we observe similar performance until 2015–2016, when Vietnam surpasses a failing Mozambique. This corresponds to a dramatic fall in FDI inflow for Mozambique from 2013 through 2017. The RENAMO insurgency (2013–2019) and insurgencies by Islamist groups (2015 to present) perhaps explain this drop in FDI. Mozambique is three times poorer than Vietnam and suffers from more serious corruption. In spite of considerable foreign aid as well as astronomical inflows of foreign direct investment—twice that of Vietnam, it did not surpass Vietnam in GDP per capita growth, and industry (including construction) remains under 25% of GDP.

The investment from abroad financed international trade, and Vietnam has become a trading country, with total trade being the equivalent of 210% of GDP in 2019 and increasing (see Fig. 2.4). It placed 56th world-wide in 2018 (2019 data was not available for many countries at the time of redaction), but 14 of the top 15 countries had a population under 5 million, and only a handful of the top 55 (such as Iran, South Korea, Tanzania, Somalia and South Sudan) had a population over 10 million. Figure 2.5 reveals that first decade of the current century was marked by a dramatic trade deficit, but the trade balance gradually has become positive since that time.

The growth in Vietnam has made a few billionaires and there is an emerging wealthy class. It is also true that a portion of the population is under the poverty line. Nonetheless, Vietnam has reported a GINI coefficient[1] about 0.34 for the past ten years, increasing in the past five, reaching 0.357 in 2018. This is the lowest in the region with the exception of Myanmar's 0.307 in 2017, a statistic which may be suspect, or simply the result of widespread impoverishment. Labour income share of GDP was 40% in Vietnam, compared to 26% in the Philippines and 44% in Thailand. Figure 2.6 manifests a clear and dramatic decrease in

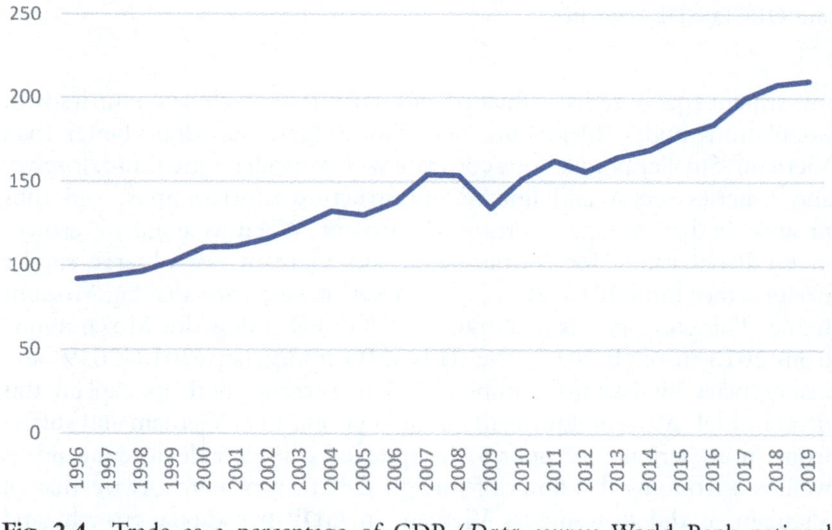

Fig. 2.4 Trade as a percentage of GDP (*Data sources* World Bank national accounts data, and OECD National Accounts data files)

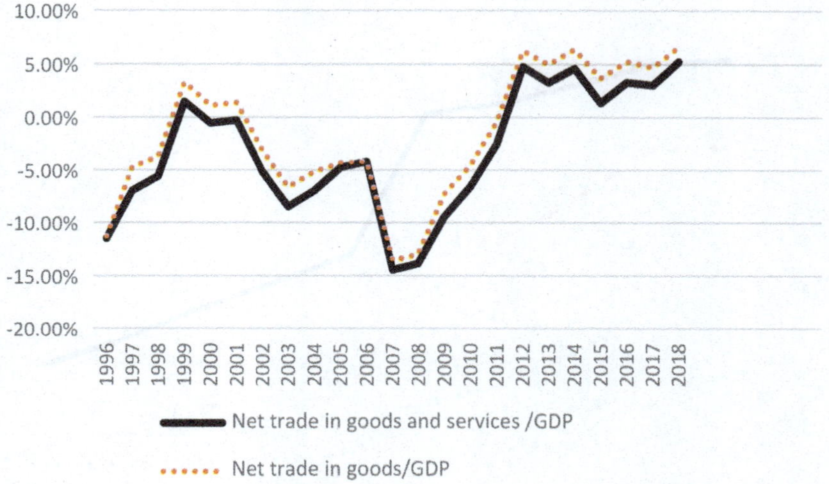

Fig. 2.5 Net Trade of Vietnam (*Data source* International Monetary Fund, Balance of Payments Statistics Yearbook and data files)

poverty headcount in Vietnam since 1996—although the trend must be interpreted warily due to changing estimates of purchasing power parity exchange rates. What poverty remains is still very real and is 70% concentrated among ethnic minorities living in highland areas with limited transport and communications.

In summary then, Vietnam presents an enviable record of economic progress, and this has been achieved by opening the economy to international trade and foreign capital.

Analysis of the Production and Expenditure Sides of GDP and GDP Growth

Production Side Analysis

Figure 2.7 reveals an unsurprising structure of GDP by sectors, with services to industry to agriculture, fisheries and forestry in roughly 6 to 5 to 2 ratios. The importance of industry did decrease somewhat from 2004 to 2010, somewhat in keeping with Rodrik's (2016) observation of premature industrialisation in many developing economies due to globalisation; however, the decrease is far less dramatic than the case of the

Fig. 2.6 Poverty headcount ratio at various daily income cut-off points in 2011 PPP US dollars. Figures in percent of total of population (*Data source* World Bank, Development Research Group. Data are based on primary household survey data obtained from government statistical agencies and World Bank country departments)

Philippines, an economy relatively isolated from globalisation. Also, the World Bank data show an upward trend since 2010. Table 2.1 uses the more detailed data of the General Statistics Office of Vietnam to confirm a weakening of industry in general and manufacturing in particular coinciding with the global financial crisis, but also that manufacturing alone accounts for 25% of the growth in GDP since 2005, 30% of the growth since 2010 and 35% of growth since 2015. The next chapter will show the opposite to be true for the Philippines, so we have a clear counterexample to any surmise that globalisation causes premature industrialisation. What this counter example suggests is that the there are other factors that should be taken into account, most notably the effective economic policy of each country with regards to FDI and industry.

Employment moved out of agriculture (an employment category including agriculture, hunting, forestry and fishing as well) was evenly

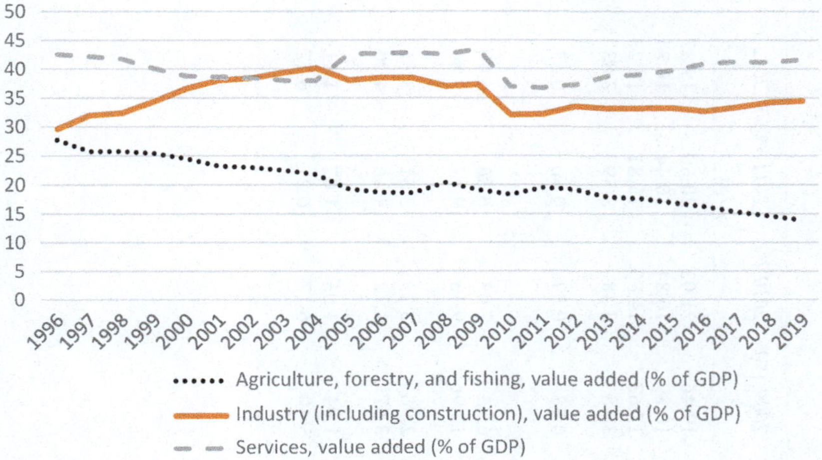

Fig. 2.7 Production composition of GDP (*Data source* World Bank national accounts data, and OECD National Accounts data files)

split by services and industry, although there is a trend for more men than women to move out of agriculture, and for more of these men to move into industry while more women moved into services. Agriculture accounted for 36.4% of employment in 2020, services for 35.2% and industry for the remaining 29.4%. Although the higher number of workers in services allows them to account for a bigger portion of GDP than industry, it is also true that labour productivity, the value added per worker in services, is only marginally lower than that in industry. Neither services nor manufacture have high domestic value added, since sophisticated services are underdeveloped (and educational and research services underpaid), while much manufacture is assembly of foreign value-added parts. Minh (2020) notes that much FDI has been into low value-added work.[2] Although Baum and Dabla-Norris (2020) noted that 'low- or zero-tariff imports combined with surging FDI enabled first low-tech manufacturing exports and later exports of more complex high-tech goods', this does not mean that Vietnam has 'high-tech' manufacturing and should not be confused with a move up the value chain. Assembling parts into the tight space of a smartphone may be tricky and require a controlled environment, but does not have the value added of the manufacture of such parts as the accelerometer, the display, the camera or

Table 2.1 Breakdown of economic activities

Economic activities contributing to GDP	*2005 (%)*	*2006 (%)*	*2007 (%)*	*2008 (%)*	*2009 (%)*	*2010 (%)*	*2011 (%)*	*2012 (%)*
Agriculture, forestry and fishing	21.58	20.94	20.32	20.13	19.46	21.02	20.50	19.87
Mining and quarrying	13.37	12.25	11.18	10.18	10.39	10.84	10.44	10.34
Manufacturing	15.66	16.59	17.40	18.08	17.63	14.80	15.81	16.23
Electricity, gas, stream and air conditioning supply	2.82	2.90	2.95	3.07	3.18	3.48	3.59	3.83
Water supply, sewerage, waste management and remediation activities	0.51	0.51	0.52	0.53	0.53	0.59	0.60	0.62
Construction	5.76	5.98	6.26	5.90	6.24	7.03	6.56	6.40
Wholesale and retail trade; repair of motor vehicles and motorcycles	12.18	12.35	12.55	12.68	12.96	9.15	9.47	9.84
Transportation and storage	2.54	2.61	2.72	2.88	2.96	3.29	3.31	3.31
Accommodation and food service activities	3.32	3.49	3.67	3.78	3.67	4.12	4.16	4.20
Information and communication	0.92	0.94	0.97	1.02	1.04	1.05	1.07	1.11
Financial, banking and insurance activities	4.89	4.95	5.03	5.24	5.40	6.17	6.21	6.17

Economic activities contributing to GDP	*2005 (%)*	*2006 (%)*	*2007 (%)*	*2008 (%)*	*2009 (%)*	*2010 (%)*	*2011 (%)*	*2012 (%)*
Real estate activities	6.64	6.64	6.51	6.49	6.43	6.98	6.78	6.47
Professional, scientific and technical activities	1.42	1.40	1.38	1.36	1.34	1.48	1.48	1.49
Administrative and support service activities	0.41	0.40	0.40	0.40	0.40	0.42	0.42	0.42
Activities of Communist Party, socio-political organisations; public administration and defense; compulsory security	2.43	2.45	2.47	2.49	2.53	2.92	2.93	2.96
Education and training	2.19	2.22	2.25	2.30	2.33	2.66	2.67	2.70
Human health and social work activities	1.03	1.04	1.05	1.07	1.09	1.24	1.24	1.26
Arts, entertainment and recreation	0.64	0.65	0.65	0.67	0.69	0.77	0.78	0.78
Other service activities	1.55	1.56	1.57	1.58	1.59	1.82	1.81	1.81
Activities of households as employers; undifferentiated goods and services producing activities of households for own use	0.15	0.15	0.15	0.15	0.16	0.16	0.16	0.16
Total of all activities except taxes and subsidies	1,588,647	1,699,504	1,820,665	1,923,748	2,027,590	1,887,083	2,016,129	2,140,840

(continued)

Table 2.1 (continued)

Economic activities contributing to GDP	*2013 (%)*	*2014 (%)*	*2015 (%)*	*2016 (%)*	*2017 (%)*	*2018 (%)*
Agriculture, forestry and fishing	19.37	18.95	18.17	17.34	16.69	16.16
Mining and quarrying	9.79	9.47	9.44	8.54	7.42	6.71
Manufacturing	16.53	16.79	17.38	18.32	19.61	20.67
Electricity, gas, stream and air conditioning supply	3.95	4.18	4.35	4.58	4.68	4.82
Water supply, sewerage, waste management and remediation activities	0.64	0.64	0.65	0.66	0.67	0.66
Construction	6.44	6.51	6.75	7.00	7.12	7.25
Wholesale and retail trade; repair of motor vehicles and motorcycles	10.02	10.24	10.45	10.66	10.81	10.94
Transportation and storage	3.32	3.31	3.25	3.25	3.28	3.30
Accommodation and food service activities	4.39	4.34	4.16	4.18	4.26	4.24
Information and communication	1.15	1.18	1.20	1.22	1.22	1.23
Financial, banking and insurance activities	6.27	6.27	6.30	6.40	6.48	6.54
Real estate activities	6.28	6.10	5.88	5.76	5.61	5.46
Professional, scientific and technical activities	1.52	1.54	1.54	1.55	1.56	1.55
Administrative and support service activities	0.43	0.44	0.43	0.44	0.44	0.44
Activities of Communist Party, socio-political organisations; public administration and defense; compulsory security	3.03	3.07	3.08	3.10	3.12	3.04
Education and training	2.77	2.82	2.82	2.85	2.87	2.86

Economic activities contributing to GDP	*2013 (%)*	*2014 (%)*	*2015 (%)*	*2016 (%)*	*2017 (%)*	*2018 (%)*
Human health and social work activities	1.29	1.31	1.31	1.32	1.33	1.33
Arts, entertainment and recreation	0.80	0.81	0.82	0.83	0.83	0.83
Other service activities	1.85	1.86	1.85	1.85	1.85	1.81
Activities of households as employers; undifferentiated goods and services producing activities of households for own use	0.16	0.16	0.16	0.16	0.16	0.16
Total of all activities except taxes and subsidies	2,254,189	2,383,427	2,546,183	2,703,764	2,889,607	3,097,783

Economic activities contributing to GDP	*Prel. 2019 (%)*	*Portion of 2005–2019 growth (%)*	*Portion of 2010–2019 growth (%)*	*Portion 2015–2019 (%)*
Agriculture, forestry and fishing	15.39	9.71	7.97	6.24
Mining and quarrying	6.34	−0.11	0.41	−3.89
Manufacturing	21.48	26.83	30.28	34.99
Electricity, gas, stream and air conditioning supply	4.92	6.84	6.81	6.77
Water supply, sewerage, waste management and remediation activities	0.67	0.81	0.77	0.73
Construction	7.38	8.87	7.85	9.46
Wholesale and retail trade; repair of motor vehicles and motorcycles	11.12	10.14	13.71	13.30
Transportation and storage	3.37	4.13	3.47	3.75
Accommodation and food service activities	4.23	5.06	4.36	4.46

(continued)

Table 2.1 (continued)

Economic activities contributing to GDP	*Prel. 2019 (%)*	*Portion of 2005–2019 growth (%)*	*Portion of 2010–2019 growth (%)*	*Portion 2015–2019 (%)*
Information and communication	1.24	1.53	1.48	1.37
Financial, banking and insurance activities	6.63	8.23	7.23	7.70
Real estate activities	5.33	4.14	3.16	3.52
Professional, scientific and technical activities	1.55	1.66	1.63	1.57
Administrative and support service activities	0.44	0.48	0.48	0.48
Activities of Communist Party, socio-political organisations; public administration and defense; compulsory security	2.96	3.44	3.00	2.56
Education and training	2.86	3.47	3.12	2.98
Human health and social work activities	1.33	1.60	1.45	1.40
Arts, entertainment and recreation	0.83	1.01	0.91	0.88
Other service activities	1.78	1.99	1.72	1.56
Activities of households as employers; undifferentiated goods and services producing activities of households for own use	0.16	0.17	0.17	0.16
Total of all activities except taxes and subsidies	3,317,357	100.00	100.00	100.00

Data source General Statistics Office of Vietnam

the processing unit, any more than do services in Vietnam add as much value as the design and marketing of smartphones. Further, smartphones are a mature industry, not an emerging one. Another potential counter example would be VinFast, the foray of VinGroup into the manufacture of high-end (compared to ventures in neighbouring countries) automobiles. Automobile assembly remains an important business and hopefully will make an important contribution to Vietnam's economic capacity, but it is a twentieth century business (Dediu 2015) that has seen the growing importance of suppliers (Kallstom 2015; Harrington 2015) and the critical elements move from overall design, assembly and sales to electronic systems and software (Fournier et al. 2011; Pelliccione et al 2017).

Expenditure Side Analysis

Figure 2.8 reveals that Vietnam ran a considerable trade deficit from the mid-1990s until the end of the global financial crisis. To some extent, investment (gross capital formation) has been the mirror image of that deficit. Domestic investment increased to compensate the decrease of foreign direct investment from 1996 to 2006, years of the Asian financial crisis and its aftermath of funds going to acquisition bargains available in neighbouring countries. Similarly, although FDI decreased by 20.5%

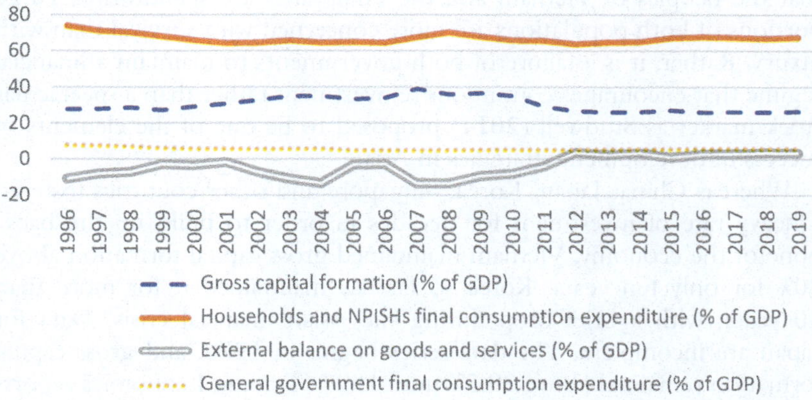

Fig. 2.8 Expenditure side components of GDP (*Data sources* World Bank national accounts data, and OECD National Accounts data files)

(in dollar figures from 2008 to 2009) at the time of the global financial crisis, gross capital formation kept increasing from 2006 through 2010. However, although both FDI and domestic investment continued to increase in absolute terms, both have stalled as a portion of GDP since 2012, with total investment remaining under 25% of GDP. Although Indonesia is the only other large economy in the region investing at this rate, this pales in comparison to the formative years of the Asian tigers that maintained investment rates above 30% for decades.

Consumption expenditure is middle of the road for the region—well below the Philippines 80%, but far above 45% that Singapore and Brunei Darussalam have limited themselves to since 2015. Government expenditure is extremely low, trending from around 8.35% of GDP in 1996 to 6.46% in 2019. In the region, only Cambodia spends a lower equivalent portion of GDP, with the governments of Singapore, Malaysia, the Philippines and Thailand spending 10% to 17% of GDP. Household expenditure is high—the Philippines are the only large economy where household consumption surpasses Vietnam as a portion of GDP, although poor and small economies of Lao and Cambodia also do so. Households in Thailand (50%), Indonesia (58%), Malaysia (increasing since 2014 from 52 up to 59%) all spend less than the 68% of Vietnam and the 73% of the Philippines. Japan at 55% and Korea at 48% as well as Singapore at 36% provide a strong contrast. However, these figures do not indicate that the peoples of Vietnam and the Philippines are spendthrifts. Large portions of both populations are more concerned with survival than with luxury. Rather, it is a failure of both governments to maintain a financial regime that encourages continuous reinvestment rather than a spectacular stock market as Studwell (2014) proposed to be one of the elements of successful development strategies in Asia.

Whereas China, Japan, Korea, Singapore and other countries fostered a heavy rate of investment for decades in order to build up the backbone of the economy, Vietnam maintained gross capital formation above 30% for only ten years. Korea so far has maintained it for more than 40 years, with a brief drop during the Asian financial crisis. Data for Japan are incomplete. The data series begins in 1970, and gross capital formation remained above 29.5% until 1997 (Trading Economics reports higher than 30% since the early 1960s, and probably this rate was maintained since the end of World War II). (For a comparison of Japan, Korean and Vietnam, see Fig. 2.9.) China has maintained a figure above 30% for 50 years, although there are probably problems with the data compiled.

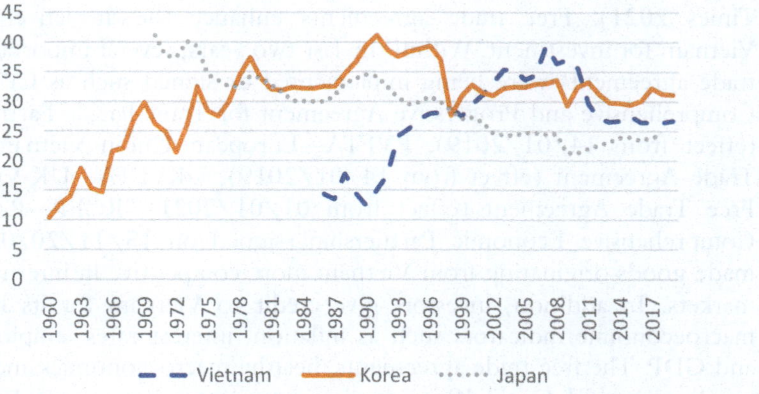

Fig. 2.9 Comparative Gross capital formation as a percentage of GDP (*Data sources* World Bank national accounts data, and OECD National Accounts data files)

Vietnam's record seems paltry. Two considerations amplify this observation: (1) the shape of the curve charting gross capital formation in Vietnam closely follows the investment bubble that preceded the global financial crisis; (2) neither Japan nor Korea had any significant foreign direct investment during their decades of high gross direct investment, and China had about one half the rate of Vietnam. If we remove the contribution of foreign direct investment, gross capital formation tops 30% for only four years, from 2003 to 2007. FDI seems to be a substitute for domestic gross capital formation rather than a complement to make investment skyrocket.

An Aperture that is Only Partly Exploited

Vietnam has been seen as a rising star in the region when it comes to attracting foreign investors thanks to its efforts to improve the investment environment, stabilise macroeconomic conditions and, most recently and as of January 2021, manage the Covid-19 pandemic successfully. Other factors such as the rising middle class, sizable market and other geopolitical advantages make it an appealing land for investment.

According to the Economic Intelligence Unit, Vietnam's FDI policy is considered to be more attractive than those of China and India (Eurasian

Times 2021). Free trade agreements enhance the attractiveness of Vietnam for investment. Within the last two years, several important free trade agreements were being implemented or signed such as CPTPP—Comprehensive and Progressive Agreement for Trans-Pacific Partnership (effect from 14/01/2019), EVFTA—European Union–Vietnam Free Trade Agreement (effect from 14/01/2019), UKVFTA—UK-Vietnam Free Trade Agreement (effect from 01/01/2021), RCEP—Regional Comprehensive Economic Partnership (signed on 15/11/2020) have made goods originating from Vietnam more competitive in international markets. In addition, investors give credit to Vietnam for its healthy macroeconomic indicators such as inflation, interest rates, employment and GDP. The free trade agreements, healthy macroeconomics and Vietnam's successful Covid-19 epidemic management have made Vietnam one of the few countries having a positive growth in both GDP and international trade in 2020 with a reasonable inflation rate at 3.2%, again reinforcing the attractiveness for investment.

As a result, the media has been reporting that investors from all over the world have invested or planned to invest in this market, including those who have long been investing in Asian markets. Investors from China have shown significantly increased interest in recent years. Before the US–China trade war, many large enterprises had a 'China-plus-1' strategy (investing in additional countries beside China), and Vietnam was often a strong candidate in that strategy. Since the outbreak of the trade war, more and more businesses want to invest in Vietnam, not only due to this strategy but also due to increasing tariff and labour costs in China. In 2020, China was the second largest source of investment in Vietnam, accounting for about 11% of all inflow. Apart from China, large ASEAN investors—such as from Singapore and Thailand—also determined to invest in Vietnam (Takahashi 2021). While a report by UNCTAD (2020) shows that foreign investment flow on a global scale decreased sharply (about 40%) in 2020, implemented FDI capital in Vietnam remained almost unchanged (Foreign Investment Agency 2020).

The trade war between the USA and China (beginning in 2017 with the talks between Donald Trump and Xi Jinping or in 2018 with the first tariffs) led to firms seeking new locations for operations outside of China, with Vietnam a likely candidate. The stage seemed set for a massive inflow of firms and capital into Vietnam, perhaps leading to a new plateau of investment in the economy. This did not happen. While some firms did re-locate to Vietnam, many preferred Singapore, Indonesia or other countries.

Vietnam has been benefitting more than any other country from the trade diversion effects of the trade war (Subbaraman et al. 2019), and also welcomed nearly half of the Japanese firms relocating production from China between April 24, 2018 and August 1, 2019 (JETRO 2020). Katakam (2019) illustrates India, Indonesia, Malaysia and Thailand as alternative Asian relocations for Japanese manufacturers. Tanakasempipat (2019) and Shukry (2019) reported that other nations also seek to welcome operations relocating from China, while Zhou and Finbarr 2019 reported that Indonesia and Malaysia benefitted from Vietnam's struggles (caused by the sudden increased demands upon roads and ports) to exploit factory relocations due to the trade war. Shehadi and Irwin (2020) give the top spot to Vietnam, but show that higher value-producing investments are going to Singapore.

FDI data for 2020 is not yet available and in any case will be skewed by the Covid-19 pandemic. What data is available shows Singapore (and India) attracting far more FDI than other ASEAN nations, with Vietnam getting less than 2/3 of Indonesia FDI, the latter country on a stronger upward trend, but for insufficient years to significantly discriminate between the two countries' success in attracting FDI.

What are the reasons for Vietnam's limited exploitation of such an opportunity? Why was Vietnam not able to absorb more of the opportunities just beyond its borders? Perceived difficulties in the conduct of business, limited sophistication and low value of production process, and insufficient infrastructure are three important weaknesses Vietnam must overcome to attain greater economic performance.

The first weakness is perceived difficulty in conducting business. Language, bureaucracy and regulations, and perhaps also fear of corruption (that does not usually impact foreign business in fact) all have made Vietnam lose ground to Singapore where English is viable in all corners of society and bureaucracy has long been streamlined to facilitate business. Vietnam has a reasonable score in the 'Ease of doing business' index (World Bank 2020), ranking 70 out of 190, but would have a better score if not dragged down by government bureaucracy in starting a business, paying taxes, importing and exporting (surprisingly, given a volume of trade more than twice GDP) and resolving insolvency. What this index does not capture, however, is the pluck of Vietnamese for business and for speaking English (that simplify business) and the real difference between Vietnamese and the languages of most other countries (that amplifies the intricacies of doing business by making it more difficult to diagnose problems and obstacles).

This is especially true in the case the private–public partnerships typical of infrastructure projects in Vietnam. For example, Ho Chi Minh City failed to find investors for 10 out of 11 public transport infrastructure projects; the single foreign investor exited by selling its participation to Vietnamese VinHomes in 2020 (Nguyen Dat 2021). Part of the problem is inconsistent laws governing such partnerships. Do et al. (2016) list 10 'most critical risk factors' in public–private transportation projects in Vietnam, of which the first three are land acquisition and compensation (surprising in a country accused of human rights abuses in land expropriation), delay in project approvals and permits and inefficient feasibility studies. These factors contributed to the third weakness, insufficient infrastructure, discussed below.

The second weakness is revealed by examining the composition of exports. This flaw also explains in part the timid level of investment because it suggests a limit upon opportunities for investment. The bulk of service trade—imports and exports—is composed of transport and travel—basically the movement of people and their luggage in and out of Vietnam. Categories of service that involved more sophisticated operations, such as finance, insurance, software and IT support, are absent. An examination of merchandise exports delivers the same message. The HS92 six-digit economic complexity metric for Vietnam in 2018 was −0.23, a rank of 79 out of 142 countries. This metric, based on data about merchandise exports and excluding services, is an attempt to measure the relative knowledge intensity of an economy. Although it is imperfect as a measure of the sophistication of services (see Macdonald 2019), this reinforces the notion that Vietnam is not mobilizing knowledge to develop higher value products and services.

Researchers at Duke University, perhaps borrowing from the notions of supply chains and value chains from business management doctrine, have proposed dividing international trade into two categories: traditional trade composed of imports and exports between two countries, and global value chains involving the transfer of value across at least two distinct national frontiers and thus involving at least three different countries. This simple distinction is important for two reasons. First, global value chain trade is more than half of all international trade, and its proportion is growing. Second, there is a correlation between higher national income and greater participation in global value chains. This second reason is somewhat problematic, however. Richer countries usually have a higher number of more powerful companies who can extract more value from a value chain than less influential firms, so participation alone is not a guarantor of success. Vietnam is a case in point. Vietnam does participate in global value chains, but has been unable either to climb the value ladder (moving to more sophisticated contributions in the chain) or to develop local support industries to further expand production in the chains in which Vietnam is present. This latter leaves Vietnam vulnerable to transfer pricing tactics (the head office in the home country sets high prices for imports into the host country) that reduce the capital retained in the country.

An issue of concern for the coming years is that additive manufacturing and robotics will erode the labour cost advantages in emerging markets such as Vietnam, while supply chain digitalisation will demand more sophistication for GVC participation. Mid-sized businesses in Vietnam will need to become more aggressive to obtain funding either from FDI or domestic banks, in order to upgrade their operations for export (see Nguyen 2020 for more detail).

Two sets of factors contribute to this situation with Vietnam on the side lines of the knowledge economy: institutional and cultural impediments to the knowledge economy on the one hand, and separation of intrinsic motivation and success on the other (see Stiglitz 1999).

Institutional and cultural impediments. The current role of tertiary education in Vietnam's economy and society slows the change to a knowledge economy. Vietnam performs well in primary and secondary education, but tertiary institutions fall short. The reason is not the innate talent of Vietnamese professors—although some academics do arrive at their position through corruption rather than knowledge—but because of the manner in which tertiary institutions are financed. Virtually all funding comes from government and is tied to students-hours taught. As a result, professors teach 500–600 hours a year, about triple the rate in OECD countries. Many professors have outside jobs to make ends meet. As a consequence, research is very modest and often perfunctory (although, remarkably, Vietnamese academics publish more than their counterparts in the Philippines and Indonesia—Nguyen and Pham 2011), and teaching is done from textbooks with little personal input. One case in point is business law taught in English (the prestigious business schools teach in English rather than Vietnamese, as an added attraction): business law of Australia, Canada, the UK or the United States will be learned instead of Vietnamese business law, with some local addenda as foreign professors glean bits of information although they usually cannot read or speak Vietnamese. Thus, business and economics formation is even more theoretical in Vietnam than in OECD countries. Something analogous happens in engineering courses. To become an effective socialist-oriented market economy in the twenty-first century, Vietnam must abandon the nineteenth century version of Marxism where university professors are functionaries parroting the official ideology of whomever is currently overseeing the state. The present situation, combined with presence of some incompetent academics bribing their way to high profile positions, has led businesses either to eschew loftier ambitions of climbing the value chain or else, in the case of businesses with deeper pockets, to have recourse to foreign consulting firms with imperfect knowledge of Vietnam. Local consulting firms are not numerous enough for the needs of businesses, especially mid-sized businesses, nor are always of high quality (see JICA 2019). Business and technical recipes for success are copied to Vietnam instead of being digested and then re-invented by Vietnamese for Vietnam's economy.

Intrinsic motivation and success. The move to a knowledge-based economy implies a flatter hierarchical structure—at least as regards operations, given that both Korea and Japan are successful in the knowledge economy while maintaining an authoritarian organisational culture. This flatter structure is only possible when personal and organisational success are linked to the intrinsic motivation of a job well done. If personal advancement depends more upon personal loyalties and drinking with the boss or customers, as is frequent in Vietnam, that link is at risk.

The third weakness is inadequate infrastructure—roads, rail, bridges, tunnels and ports. A sudden dramatic increase in the volume of manufacturing would test current logistic capacity of any nation; however, development requires that a nation anticipates growth by investment in infrastructure. Good infrastructure may seem as the result of wealth, but it is also a pre-requisite for producing wealth. Vietnam simply was not ready. Although the country did an admirable job in recovering the road and rail network from long decades of destructive war, and also has built airports and improved seaports, the basic system has not really changed since colonial days beyond the constructions of airports. Although the large cities of Vietnam do not suffer from horrendous traffic jams like those of Jakarta, Manila and Bangkok, this is not because of generous urban planning and an effective public transport system as is the case of Singapore. It is because until the present time only a small portion of the population has been able to afford cars. Vietnam has not invested enough money to increase the efficiency of logistics within the country and across borders. The cost of transportation is not high as a fraction of GDP—transportation and storage accounted for less than three percent of the country's total GDP in 2019, almost the lowest ratio in the world. Rolling stock and roads, rails and bridges are mostly long since amortised and drivers have modest salaries. However, the network for transport is insufficient, inefficient because poorly connected and burdened with bottlenecks, slowing the transfer of goods, thus raising inventory costs, missing markets and limiting the economic scale of factories and warehouses. As a result, comprehensive logistics costs surpass 20% of GDP (see Nguyen et al. 2020, Section 4.4.6), and it is this high ratio, not the low salaries and almost free equipment, that is embedded in the structure of business costs, discouraging new investment.

The next section examines this infrastructure challenge in greater detail.

Infrastructure Development in Vietnam

There have been existing challenges as the road and port infrastructure lags behind increased export intent within the country, resulting in traffic congestion and lengthened delays at the ports (Thanh Thom 2020). A national highway system that connects the key air and seaports in the country is not in place (Tri Vo 2020). Forecasts also show that Vietnam may face an energy shortage in the near future, with demand for electricity exceeding its supply by 6.6 billion kilowatt hours in 2021 (Khanh Vu 2019). These infrastructure challenges, if not properly addressed, may discourage future investors and thus affect the ambition of this nation to overcome the middle-income trap, becoming a developed country with a per capita income over 20 thousand USD by 2045.

According to the latest report on infrastructure of World Economic Forum (2019), Vietnam was in the lower half of its overall ranking,

77th among 141 countries in the study. Transport infrastructure alone ranked higher than the overall rating at 67th position. Looking into the detailed criteria for the overall ranking (see Table 2.2), there are 4 issues that need immediate improvement in transport infrastructure in Vietnam, including road connectivity, quality of road infrastructure, efficiency of air transport services and efficiency of seaport services. All of these four criteria are below the average if compared with all countries included in the survey.

Vietnam has made significant improvements over the past three decades, especially in telecommunications and transport and logistics. However, the current status of transport and logistics limits the potential of this country at its current level of development. The subsequent analysis will provide explanations in terms of quantity and quality of

Table 2.2 Vietnam infrastructure rankings

	International ranking	*Trend improving (+), degrading (-) or steady (=)*
Overall infrastructure	77th	+
Transport infrastructure	67th	+
Road connectivity	104th	+
Quality of road infrastructure	103rd	+
Railroad density	58th	+
Efficiency of train services	54th	+
Airport connectivity	22nd	=
Efficiency of air transport services	103rd	+
Liner shipping connectivity	19th	+
Efficiency of seaport services	83rd	+

Data source World Economic Forum (2019)

investment in infrastructure on Vietnam over the past two decades with a focus on transport and logistics infrastructure.

Quantity of Investment

Investment in infrastructure development in Vietnam has been significant over the past two decades when measured in terms of share of the national GDP. In the period 1995–2007, the average investment was a remarkable 10% of GDP (Nguyen and Dapice 2009). Although this high level of investment was not maintained for the following period, the average rate of investment during the period 2008–2017 is also considerable, at 6.45% per year (see Fig. 2.10). If calculating for all 22 years (1995–2017), the average investment was 8.45% of GDP. This is a high rate of infrastructure investment, only lower than the economic tigers of Asia such as Taiwan and South Korea in their peak development period but higher than other ASEAN countries.

The infrastructure investment is a large percentage of the GDP of this relatively small-sized economy. When compared with the regional countries in Asia, Fig. 2.11 shows that in 2008–2017, Vietnam shows

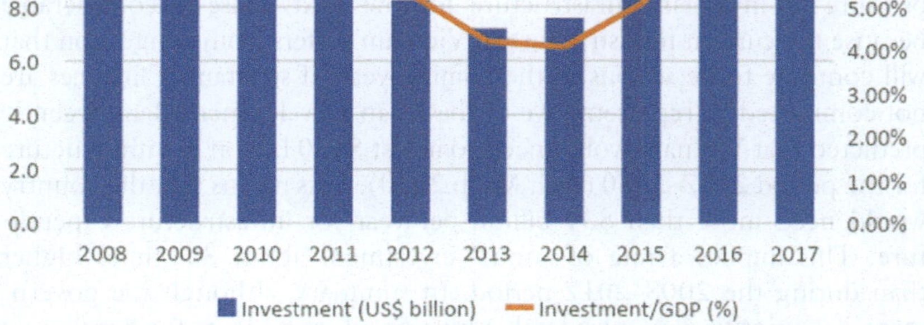

Fig. 2.10 Infrastructure investment in Vietnam (*Data source* Global Infrastructure Hub [2021])

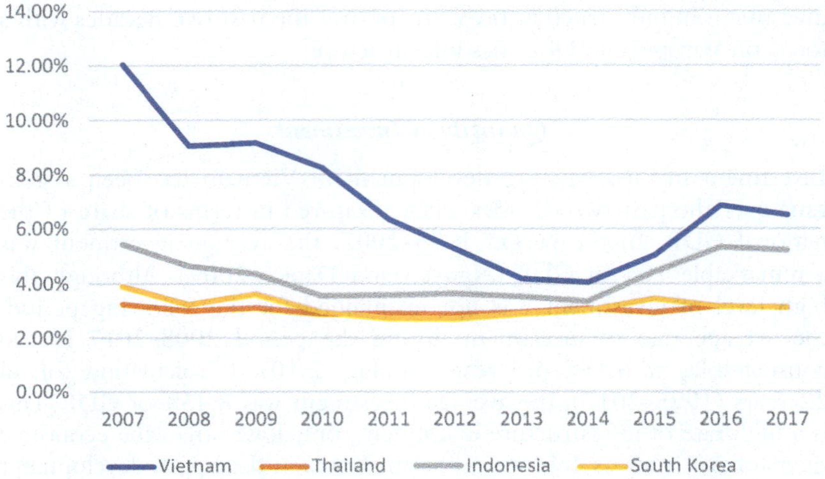

Fig. 2.11 Infrastructure investment of Vietnam and selected countries in Asia as a percentage of GDP (*Data source* Global Infrastructure Hub [2021])

a high investment-to-GDP ratio which outperformed most other comparable Asian counterparts. Unfortunately, in dollar value terms, the above investment was still quite limited and has not met the development needs of the economy.

The annual average expenditure on infrastructure in Vietnam in 2008–2017 was under $10 billion, which is lower than the requirements of sustainable development of the economy. Therefore, the pressure to invest in infrastructure for the next phase is considerable because the current infrastructure in Vietnam suffers from congestion that will continue to be serious in the coming years if substantial finances are not committed. A representative of the Asian Development Bank recently predicted that Vietnam would need to invest $450 billion in infrastructure for the period 2017–2030 (Anh Minh 2020). This means that the country would need more than $34 billion per year for infrastructure expenditure. This implies a rate of annual investment about 3.5 times higher than during the 2008–2017 period. In summary, although the government has prioritised a considerable portion of its budgets for developing infrastructure over the past two decades, Vietnam still needs to invest more to maintain its rate of economic development, in the view of the Asian Development Bank.

Efficiency of Investment

In addition to this shortfall, those limited funds could have been invested far more efficiently. One of the commonly used metrics to measure the efficiency of investment capital is the ICOR (Incremental Capital – Output Ratio). ICOR shows the number of additional units of capital required to produce a new unit of output. Thus, the higher the ICOR of an economy, the more inefficient the use capital. Vietnam's ICOR over time shows that the country has not been using the investment capital efficiently. One previous study shows that it was much higher than other East Asian countries (Nguyen and Dapice 2009). More recently, over 2008–2017, the ICOR has been even worse than the earlier period (see Table 2.3).

Noteworthy is the ICOR of the state economic sector. This sector has a very high ICOR at 10.28 in 2012–2017, reflecting a remarkably inefficient usage of investment. The problem is that it is precisely state-owned enterprises that are engaged in Vietnam's infrastructure, either investing alone or, more frequently, seeking private partners, both domestic and foreign. The result is a huge expenditure of resources costing Vietnam's productivity. The productivity of capital in the Vietnamese economy is among the lowest in the world. This is a steep hurdle for Vietnam's growth in the long term. In addition, Vietnam's investment in recent years has also relied on external loans, which means that the country is shifting its future demand to the present (since future demand capacity will be used to pay interest). Borrowing for investment can leverage an economy if the loans are used effectively and efficiently to facilitate the business environment, boost demand and increase income for

Table 2.3 ICOR in Vietnam

	ICOR
Vietnam 1997–2007	5.1
Vietnam 2008–2017	6.3
State economic sector (2012–2017)	10.28

Data source General Statistics Office of Vietnam (2018) and CIEM (2019)

the people. A poor investment efficiency, however, will be a burden on the economy and for the next generation if the loans are not transformed into higher productivity.

Project Quality, Governance and Corruption

The quality of infrastructure projects is often problematic in Vietnam. There have been many scandals about the quality and cost overrun in large infrastructure projects. The most recent example would be the expressway project connecting the two central provinces of Vietnam, the Danang–Quang Ngai Expressway. This project has a total investment capital of $1.6 billion from JICA, WB and reciprocal capital, managed by the VEC (Vietnam Expressway Corporation), a state-owned company under the Ministry of Transportation. The highway went under construction starting mid-2013. In September 2018, the expressway was put into operation after more than 5 years of construction. In early October 2018, just one month later, many locations on the expressway had peeled, with holes appearing (Dac Thanh and Nguyen Dong 2018). Poor supervision and corruption were later discovered which result in many officials and leaders being brought to court.

Similarly, the operation of infrastructure projects after completion has also seen several cases of corruption which cause huge loss of tax revenue and prolong the charging time, notably in the case of the HCMC–Trung Luong highway, connecting Ho Chi Minh City and neighbouring provinces of Long An and Tien Giang, in the south of Vietnam. The contractor used his personal relationship with the leadership of Ministry of Transport to win the bid and then manipulated software, causing a total loss of VND 725 billion (equivalent to $31.7 million). The case was uncovered in 2018 and at the end of 2020, the former heads of the Ministry, including former Ministers and vice Ministers, faced charges and suffered a total penalty of nearly 15 years in jail.

In 2017, many people across the country were shocked with the wrong placement of the Cai Lay toll road. This toll booth officially was operated since August 2017, but it was halted after two weeks of operation because of the rare fierce opposition of people and drivers. Usually in Vietnam, there is very little tolerance for dissidents and the government often acts very quickly with any signs of public dissatisfaction. However, in this case it is evident that there were certain concessions by the government. Specifically, the government halted toll collection after protesting drivers caused prolonged congestion, instead of suppressing the unrest (Mi Nguyen 2017). It is commonly believed that the location of the toll booth was misplaced, meaning that vehicles had to pay fees even if they did not use the road. The investor claimed that they also repaired the old road on which the toll road was built, but the residents and drivers pointed out that these repairs cost very little and they already paid for the costs via other channels. In Vietnam, the private investors for public private infrastructure projects are often appointed rather than selected among competing parties (Le Kien 2019). This practice can give rise to the selection of incompetent private partners, resulting in waste and losses.

In addition to this corruption, poor project management has caused many infrastructure projects to suffer huge cost overruns and multiple delays with both financial and opportunity costs. The two metro projects in Hanoi and Ho Chi Minh City are the typical examples. In the north of Vietnam, the Cat Linh–Ha Dong railway project in Hanoi was projected to be constructed from 2008 to 2013. However, by the end of 2020, the metro has not yet been put into commercial operation. Going through several adjustments, by 2019, the total investment increased by more than 205% to 18,000 billion VND from the original VND 8,770 billion (an increase of VND 9231 billion, equivalent to about $400 million) (Ngoc Ha 2019). In the south of Vietnam, Ho Chi Minh City, Ben Thanh–Suoi Tien railway project, connecting the city centre and the eastern part of the city, manifested similar problems and results. The total initial investment of the approved project in 2007 was $1.091 billion. By 2018, the total expected investment was adjusted to approximately $2.5 billion (VND 47,325 billion) (Ha Vu 2019). Initially, the project had been expected to be completed and put into commercial use in 2017. In 2018, commencement of operations was pushed back to 2020, but this new deadline was apparently not feasible. The common reasons provided for the delays and cost increase are the fluctuations in input costs, exchange rates and changes in policy. Although never specifically acknowledged, in the final analysis it is poor project management that caused these problems.

Capital for Infrastructure Investment

Experience from other countries suggests that private sector participation in infrastructure development is essential to ensure the quality and number of infrastructure projects for sustainable social–economic development.

India and Brazil are the two examples where inadequate investment results in growth below potential while China is the opposite. This explains different growth across these countries (Spencer 2015). The government of Vietnam has set ambitious goals of high and sustainable development over the next two decades. Therefore, one of the prerequisites must be a sustainable investment in infrastructure. But there is always a gap between the investment need and the available government funding sources, especially in countries with weak financial discipline and poor accountability. Most infrastructure projects are large, with capital needs that require the participation of the private sector. This is why the public–private partnership (PPP) is often a popular choice in many countries (ADB 2014).

However, Vietnam is facing many obstacles before this popular form of investment can be truly effective. Vietnam has 336 PPP projects signed by the end of 2019. Of these, there are 140 BOT (Build-Operate-Transfer) projects, 188 BT (Build-Transfer) projects and 8 projects applying other types of contracts. The total mobilised capital to invest in the development of the national infrastructure system is about US$69.6 billion (Le Kien 2019). PPP projects have positively contributed to improving the quantity and quality of transport infrastructure in Vietnam. Infrastructure projects such as energy, urban infrastructure, wastewater and treatment have promptly met urgent needs of the people for public services and urgent infrastructure needs.

The problem is that PPP projects are often implemented slowly and at great cost. Some large projects have had to be stopped and transformed back to public-investment type projects or have to be terminated after a long period of inactivity. Two typical examples are the My Thuan–Can Tho Expressway project, which has just been converted from BOT to public investment by Prime Minister Nguyen Xuan Phuc. Similarly, the project that connects the East–West Highway of Ho Chi Minh City and Ho Chi Minh City–Trung Luong Expressway has been also proposed for termination because of contractor problems.

Towards a Modern Infrastructure for Sustainable Development: Challenges Ahead

Maintaining an average expenditure of 8.45% of GDP on infrastructure during 23 years in 1995–2017 is an acknowledged effort of succeeding Vietnamese government leaders to develop needed infrastructure and has been an important growth engine for Vietnam through the past three decades. Despite the great economic achievements, challenges are ahead. Apart from the problems of poor project quality, problematic project management and corruption, other challenges will be briefly discussed below.

The first challenge is the weak connectivity of transport infrastructure in Vietnam. The peculiar geography of Vietnam bequeaths it a long shape, narrow width and a long coastline. Across the country, sea is bordered by the highland, mountainous areas or complicated river systems. This creates challenges in developing transport and energy infrastructure, especially those projects that connect different regions in the country. However, the long coastline and rivers are an advantage in building the intermodal transport connections. Vietnam has not fully exploited its potential while still struggling to deal with infrastructure challenges as presented above. Currently, logistics costs in Vietnam are among the highest in the world (accounting for 20.9% of GDP), much higher than India at 13% and Brazil (12%) (Nguyen et al. 2020). India has similar wealth and population density levels to Vietnam. Logistic costs relative to GDP are even 25% higher than in Russia (Armstrong & Associates 2020); the country with the largest land area in the world and a far lower population density than Vietnam, more than compensating for the greater GDP. Various studies show that the quality and level of transport infrastructure is uneven across the country and is often threatened by natural disasters such as typhoons and floods. A number of international and domestic trade corridors are increasingly congested while other components remain inefficient or underdeveloped (Oh et al. 2019). The Mekong Delta region is a typical example. This is the largest agriculture producer in Vietnam and is home to about 20% of the country's population, but its infrastructure is among the weakest in the country. Therefore, it is recommended that the Vietnamese government overcome this important barrier by developing multimodal transport facilities (that accommodate several of truck, rail, other land, perhaps also air and water transport) (Cuu Long 2020).

Secondly, there may be less manoeuvring room in fiscal policies for the coming time and this could have a negative impact on state budget for infrastructure building. Vietnam is widely integrated with the global economy, so global economic instability and a significant decline in aggregate demand due to the pandemic and subsequent re-adjustment of supply chains will have an unpredictable but probably negative impact on Vietnam's economy in spite of the internal economic readiness of the economy throughout most of 2020. If abnormal conditions continue, tax revenue could decline in the coming years while spending for urgent matters such as bailout packages have to be maintained. In addition, since 2016 Vietnam has graduated from ODA (Official Development Assistance) which used to provide soft loans infrastructure investment in Vietnam over the past three decades.

On the anti-corruption front, Vietnam has shown a strong determination to fight corruption in past years, but it needs to deploy stronger measures than is currently the case. The corruption perception index of Vietnam is still very high (ranked 96 out of 180 countries) (Transparency International 2020), while salaries in the public sector remain very low and the accountability of top party officials is not yet regulated in any law, a formula for corruption. These problems hinder private investments in infrastructure such as PPP projects.

Conclusion

Since the America-led embargo ended in 1994, Vietnam has opened up its markets to investment in international trade and even foreign labour at the managerial and technical levels. This has led to world-leading growth, as Vietnam has been consistently among the top 5 fastest growing economies of large populations, providing a clear illustration of how openness to capital, trade (and, although less discussed, labour) facilitates the development of an economy by using the wealth of other nations, in the forms of capital and demand, to increase the value-producing capacity of labour and natural resources. In spite of such strong results, Vietnam is still performing below its potential and needs to exploit openness even more. A free-market ideologue may prefer for things to happen'naturally', but there are factors and interests skewing the market in any economy, including Vietnam's, so market freedom cannot increase without appropriate government action. A short shopping list of government intervention includes:

- Diverting more funds to factors that facilitate business success such as physical infrastructure.
- Tweaking the financial regime to increase domestic capital formation, such as taxing dividends and profits made on the stock market, or giving tax breaks for investment in machinery and equipment.
- Dealing with corruption—although this is not usually a problem for foreign businesses (enterprise surveys) it clearly has been a problem when foreigners become bemired in public projects.
- Requiring technology transfer and domestic supply as part of FDI projects.
- Improving the effort to move up the value chain through
  - Better support for tertiary education
  - Encouraging a science-based culture among businesses, including in the financial sector
  - Carrying out industry studies to strategise upgrading in select value chains.

Notes

1. The GINI coefficient, ratio or score may be reported on 100 or on 1.0, is a measure of dispersion that indicates inequality of income. A higher score indicates greater inequality. OECD scores vary from the relatively egalitarian Slovenia (.236) to the unequal Costa Rica (.488). Switzerland has a score of .299; the U.S.A. .390. The World Bank report slightly different scores.
2. Minh 2020 found that FDI has a negative effect upon GDP growth in Vietnam, and observes that this 'negative effect of FDI could be explained by the fact that Vietnam is a labour-intensive economy and almost FDI invested into Vietnam comes from investors who are looking for low-cost and low-skill labour force. Accordingly, the FDI enterprises locate the low added-value stages of production such as assembling, processing and manufacturing in Vietnam and leave a modest profit to the domestic economy'. Chapter 1 dealt with the inconsistent results of such empirical work into the relation between FDI and economic growth.

References

ADB. 2014. A Comparative Infrastructure Development Assessment of the Republic of Korea and the Kingdom of Thailand. Manila, Philippines: The Asian Development Bank. Retrieved from https://www.adb.org/sites/default/files/publication/100117/comparative-infrastructure-development-kor-tha.pdf

ADB. 2017. ASEAN Corporate Governance Scorecard Country Reports and Assessments 2015. Manila, Philippines: The Asian Development Bank and ASEAN Capital Markets Forum.

Akhlaque, A., A.B.C. Ong Lopez, and A. Coste. 2018. *Vietnam: Enhancing Enterprise Competitiveness and SME Linkages—Lessons from International and Environment: Evidence from an SME Survey in 2015*. Hanoi: Central Institute for Economic Management of Vietnam.

An Chi. 2018. State-Owned Enterprises Operate Inefficiently Despite Large Resources. Retrieved from https://theleader.vn/doanh-nghiep-nha-nuoc-hoat-dong-kem-hieu-qua-du-nguon-luc-lon-1541562951343.htm Accessed January 25, 2021.

Anh Minh. 2020. Sharing Experiences in Developing Effective PPP Infrastructure in Vietnam. Retrieved from http://baochinhphu.vn/Kinh-te/Chia-se-kinh-nghiem-phat-trien-ha-tang-PPP-hieu-qua-o-Viet-Nam/385251.vgp. Accessed January 25, 2021.

ASEAN-Japan Center. 2020. Global Value Chains in ASEAN – Paper 11: Viet Nam. Tokyo: ASEAN-Japan Center. Retrieved from https://www.asean.or.jp/ja/wp-content/uploads/sites/2/GVC_Viet-Nam_Paper-11_full_web.pdf. Accessed January 25, 2021.

Armstrong & Associates. 2020. Global Third-Party Logistics (3PL) Market Estimates. Available at https://www.3plogistics.com/3pl-market-info-resources/3pl-market-information/global-3pl-market-size-estimates/.

Asia Regional Integration Center. 2018. Free Trade Agreements. Retrieved from https://aric.adb.org/database/fta. Accessed January 25, 2021.

Baum, Anja, and Era Dabla-Norris. 2020. Vietnam's Development Success Story and the Unfinished SDG Agenda. IMF. Available at https://www.elibrary.imf.org/view/journals/001/2020/031/article-A001-en.xml.

Capling, A., and J. Ravenhill. 2011. Multilateralising Regionalism: What Role for the Trans-Pacific Partnership Agreement? *The Pacific Review* 24 (5): 553–575.

CIEM. 2019. State Economy, SOE Restructuring: Evaluate the Implementation Results in the Period 2011–2020 and Propose Solutions for the Period 2021–2030. Hanoi: The Central Institute for Economic Management. Retrieved from http://st.aus4reform.org.vn/staticFile/Subject/2020/04/27/sach-_ktnn-va-tai-co-cau-ktnn_da-sua_271636555.pdf. Accessed January 25, 2021.

CIEM, ILSSA, and UNU-WIDER. 2016. Characteristics of the Vietnamese Business

Cuu Long. 2020. More than 1.3 Million People in the Mekong Delta Migrated. VnExpress. Retrieved from https://vnexpress.net/hon-1-3-trieu-dan-mien-tay-di-cu-4206243.html Accessed January 25, 2021.

Dac Thanh, and Nguyen Dong. 2018. The First Highway in the Central Region Appeared Many Potholes. Retrieved from https://vnexpress.net/cao-toc-dau-tien-o-mien-trung-xuat-hien-nhieu-o-ga-3821327.html.

Dang, L.N., and A.T. Chuc. 2019. Challenges in Implementing the Credit Guarantee Scheme for Small and Medium-Sized Enterprises: The Case of Viet Nam. ADBI Working Paper Series (No. 941).

Dediu, Horace. 2015. The Entrant's Guide to The Automobile Industry. Asymco. Available at http://www.asymco.com/2015/02/23/the-entrants-guide-to-the-automobile-industry/. Accessed January 26, 2021.

Do, Tien Sy, Veerasak Likhitruangsilp, Masamitsu Onishu, and Phong Thanh Nguyen. 2016. Impacts of Risk Factors on the Performance of Public-Private Partnership Transportation Projects in Vietnam. *ASEAN Engineering Journal Part C* 6 (1): 2–24.

Foreign Investment Agency. 2020. Foreign Investment in 2020. Retrieved from https://fia.mpi.gov.vn/Detail/CatID/457641e2-2605-4632-bbd8-39ee65454a06/NewsID/a590e4ad-2ba7-48d7-af1e-7b613542fea3. Accessed January 25, 2021.

Fournier, Guy, Henning Hinderer, Daniel Schmid, René Seign, and Manuel Baumann. 2011. The New Mobility Paradigm: Transformation of Value Chain and Business Models, Enterprise and Work Innovation Studies, 8, IET, pp. 9–40.

General Statistics Office of Vietnam. 2018. *Results of the 2017 Economics Census*. Hanoi: Statistical Publishing House.

Global Infrastructure Hub. 2021. Investment Forecasts for Vietnam. https://outlook.gihub.org/countries/Vietnam+Thailand+Indonesia. Accessed February 3, 2021.

GSO. 2020. General Statistics Office of Vietnam.

Ha Anh. 2020. Strengthening Vietnamese Business Links to Shift Global Value Chains. Retrieved from https://dangcongsan.vn/kinh-te-va-hoi-nhap/tang-cuong-lien-ket-doanh-nghiep-viet-chuyen-dich-chuoi-gia-tri-toan-cau-566795.html. Accessed January 25, 2021.

Ha Chinh. 2020. Public Investment Disbursement Experienced the Strongest Increase in a Decade. Baochinhphu. Retrieved from http://baochinhphu.vn/Kinh-te/Giai-ngan-dau-tu-cong-tang-manh-nhat-trong-mot-thap-ky/415911.vgp. Accessed January 25, 2021.

Ha Vu. 2019. The Government Gave Three Reasons Why Metro Ben Thanh - Suoi Tien Exceeded 30 Trillion Dong in Capital. VnEconomy.

Retrieved from https://vneconomy.vn/chinh-phu-neu-ba-ly-do-khien-metro-ben-thanh-suoi-tien-doi-von-30-ngan-ty-20191103091110965.htm. Accessed January 25, 2021.

Harrington, Lisa. 2015. The Quiet Revolution: Convergence and the Future Automotive Supply Chain. DHL Supply Chain. Available at https://d3kex6ty6anzzh.cloudfront.net/uploads/2f/2f31d6a79bd581da706f937acb029de52983f18c.pdf. Accessed January 26, 2021.

Hoan, Buu. 1991. Soviet Economic Aid to Vietnam. *Contemporary Southeast Asia*. 12 (4): 360–376.

Jetro. 2020. Results of JETRO's 2019 Survey on the International Operations of Japanese Firms. Available at https://www.jetro.go.jp/en/news/releases/2020/e2740919f204387f.html. Accessed January 20, 2021.

JICA. 2019. Data Collection Survey on SME Promotion and Industrial Development in Viet Nam Final Report Japan International Cooperation Agency (JICA). Available at https://openjicareport.jica.go.jp/pdf/12334355.pdf. Accessed January 11, 2021.

Kallstrom, Henry. 2015. Suppliers' Power Is Increasing in the Automobile Industry. Market Realist. Available at https://marketrealist.com/2015/02/suppliers-power-increasing-automobile-industry/?utm_source=yahoo&utm_medium=feed&utm_content=toc-3&utm_campaign=shift-growth-global-automotive-industry. Accessed January 26, 2021.

Katakam, A. 2019. Companies Moving Production from China. *Reuters*. Available at https://graphics.reuters.com/USA-TRADE-CHINA-COMPETITION/0100B2CW1GZ/USA-TRADE-CHINA-COMPETITION.jpg. Accessed January 30, 2021.

Khanh Vu. 2019. Vietnam Will Face Severe Power Shortages from 2021: Ministry. Reuters. Retrieved from https://www.reuters.com/article/us-vietnam-energy/vietnam-will-face-severe-power-shortages-from-2021-ministry-idUSKCN1UQ11M. Accessed January 25, 2021.

Le Kien. 2019. The Government Admits That There Is Social Frustration with BOT and BT Projects. *Tuoitre*. Retrieved from https://tuoitre.vn/chinh-phu-thua-nhan-co-buc-xuc-xa-hoi-doi-voi-du-an-bot-bt-20190916163203123.htm. Accessed January 25, 2021.

Lương Bang. 2020. The Government Names Series of State-Owned Enterprises That Lost Trillion. Retrieved from https://vietnamnet.vn/vn/kinh-doanh/dau-tu/chinh-phu-diem-danh-loat-doanh-nghiep-thua-lo-nghin-ty-681097.html. Accessed January 25, 2021.

Luu Thuy. 2019. Poor Infrastructure, Unsustainable Growth. Retrieved from https://saigondautu.com.vn/kinh-te/co-so-ha-tang-kem-tang-truong-kho-ben-vung-72757.html. Accessed January 25, 2021.

Macdonald, Roderick. 2019. Appendix of Chapter 6. In *Southeast Asia and the ASEAN Economic Community*, ed. Roderick Macdonald. Cham: Palgrave Macmillan.

Mi Nguyen. 2017. Vietnam Reviews Toll Road After Rare Protests. *Reuters*. Retrieved from https://www.reuters.com/article/us-vietnam-road-idUSKBN1E2127. Accessed January 25, 2021.

Minh Nhat. 2020. How to Move FDI into Vietnam after the US-China Trade Agreement? *The Leader*. Retrieved from https://theleader.vn/dich-chuyen-fdi-vao-viet-nam-ra-sao-sau-thoa-thuan-thuong-mai-my-trung-1579233132528.htm. Accessed January 25, 2021.

Minh, Cao Hong. 2020. Remittances, Foreign Direct Investment, Imports and Economic Growth: Empirical Evidence from Vietnam. *Asian Journal of Economic Modelling* 8 (2): 133–140.

Minh Thu 2020. Current Situation and Recommendations for PPP Infrastructure Development. Retrieved from http://consosukien.vn/thuc-trang-va-kien-nghi-phat-trien-co-so-ha-tang-ppp.htm. Accessed January 25, 2021.

Ministry of Planning and Investment. 2013. Conference for 25 Years of Foreign Direct Investment in Vietnam. Hanoi: MPI. Retrieved from https://dautunuocngoai.gov.vn/_layouts/fiaportal/uploads/old_data/uploads/Doc/Ky%20yeu%2025%20nam%20DTNN_final.pdf. Accessed January 25, 2021.

Ngoc Ha. 2019. The Most Painful Project in the Capital, with a Capital of 10 Trillion Dong, 8 Times Missed Deadline. Vietnamnet. Retrieved from https://vietnamnet.vn/vn/kinh-doanh/dau-tu/duong-sat-cat-linh-ha-dong-doi-von-10-ngan-ty-8-lan-vo-tien-do-vi-sao-547853.html. Accessed January 25, 2021.

Nguyen, D.D., and F. Taghizadeh-Hesary. 2020. State-Owned Enterprise Reform in Viet Nam: Progress and Challenges. ADBI Working Paper 1071. Tokyo: Asian Development Bank Institute.

Nguyen Dat. 2021. HCMC Struggles to Attract Foreign Investors for Key Projects. VNExpress. Available at https://ampe.vnexpress.net/news/business/economy/hcmc-struggles-to-attract-foreign-investors-for-key-projects-4221137.html. Accessed January 25, 2021.

Nguyen, Q.T., C.H. Pham, and R. McClelland. 2020. Participating and Upgrading in Global Value Chains: The Case of Small and Medium Enterprises in Vietnam. In *The Economy and Business Environment of Vietnam*, ed. Roderick Macdonald, 75–92. Cham: Palgrave Macmillan.

Nguyen, Tuan V., and Ly T. Pham. 2011. Scientific Output and Its Relationship to Knowledge Economy: An Analysis of ASEAN Countries. *Scientometrics* 89: 107–117.

Nguyen, X.T., and D. Dapice. 2009. *Vietnam's Infrastructure Constraints*. Cambridge: United Nations Development Programme.

Oh, J.E., B.G. Mtonya, C. Kunaka, M.S.M. Lebrand, O. Pimhidzai, C.D. Phan, et al. 2019. Vietnam Development Report 2019: Connecting Vietnam for Growth and Shared Prosperity. The World Bank. Retrieved from https://openknowledge.worldbank.org/bitstream/handle/10986/33139/Vietnam-Development-Report-2019-Connecting-Vietnam-for-Growth-and-Shared-Prosperity.pdf?sequence=1&isAllowed=y. Accessed January 25, 2021.

Pelliccione, Patrizio, Eric Knauss, S. Rogardt Heldal, Magnus Ågren, Piergiuseppe Mallozzi, Anders Alminger, and Daniel Borgentun. 2017. Automotive Architecture Framework: The experience of Volvo Cars. *Journal of Systems Architecture* 77: 83–100.

Phang Son. 2013. Vietnam Gets Tough on State Firms in Economic Growth Push. Bloomberg News. Retrieved from https://www.bloomberg.com/news/articles/2013-07-24/vietnam-gets-tough-on-state-firms-in-economic-growth-push. Accessed January 25, 2021.

Radchenko, Sergey. 2018. Why Were the Russians in Vietnam? *The New York Times*, March 27.

Rodrik, Dani. 2016. Premature Deindustrialization. *Journal of Economic Growth* 21 (1): 1–33.

Schwab, Klaus. 2019. *The Global Competitiveness Report 2019*. Geneva: World Economic Forum.

Shehadi, Sebastian, and Alex Irwin-Hun. 2020. Asia's Busy Investors Seek Opportunities Beyond China. *Financial Times*, May 11.

Shukry, Anisah. 2019. Trade War Spurs 1,360% Investment Jump in Malaysian State. Bloomberg. Available at https://www.bloomberg.com/news/articles/2019-06-13/trade-war-spurs-1-360-investment-jump-in-this-malaysian-state. Accessed January 30, 2021.

Spencer, M. 2015. Why Public Investment? Retrieved from http://www.project-syndicate.org/commentary/public-investment-economic-growth-by-michael-spence-2015-02#xcVCiuxiQebroMSW.99. Accessed January 25, 2021.

Stiglitz, Joseph E. 1999. Public Policy for a Knowledge Economy. Presented at the Department for Trade and Industry and Center for Economic Policy Research London, UK. Available at http://citeseerx.ist.psu.edu/viewdoc/download?doi=10.1.1.123.9173&rep=rep1&type=pdf. Accessed January 11, 2021.

Studwell, Joe. 2014. *How Asia Works*. New York: Grove Press.

Subbaraman, Rob, Sonal Varma, and Michael Loo. 2019. US-China Trade Diversion: Who Benefits? Nomura. Available at https://www.nomuraconnects.com/focused-thinking-posts/us-china-trade-diversion-who-benefits/. Accessed January 25, 2021.

Takahashi, T. 2021. Thailand's Mekong Play Gives It Leg Up as Vietnam Wins Factories. Retrieved from https://asia.nikkei.com/Economy/Thailand-s-Mekong-play-gives-it-leg-up-as-Vietnam-wins-factories2#:~:text=It%20is%20illustr ated%20in%20a,also%20appear%20in%20economic%20data. Accessed January 11, 2021.

Tanakasempipat, Patpicha. 2019. Battle to Woo Trade War's Corporate Refugees Intensifies. *Reuters*. Available at https://www.reuters.com/article/usa-trade-china-competition/battle-to-woo-trade-wars-corporate-refugees-intensifies-idINKBN1WC0TF?edition-redirect=in. Accessed January 30, 2021.

Thanh Thom. 2020. Infrastructure, Manpower Hurdles to Slow Down Vietnam's Economy: Fitch Solutions. Saigontimes. Retrieved from https://english.thesaigontimes.vn/74095/infrastructure-manpower-hurdles-to-slow-down-vietnam%E2%80%99s-economy-fitch-solutions.html. Accessed January 25, 2021.

The Eurasian Times. 2021. Vietnam Beats China, India to Become Next Manufacturing Hub: Reports. Retrieved from https://eurasiantimes.com/vietnam-beats-china-india-to-become-next-manufacturing-hub-reports/. Accessed January 25, 2021.

Tran, H.T.T. 2015. Challenges of Small and Medium-Sized Enterprises (SMEs) In Vietnam during the Process of Integration into the ASEAN Economic Community (AEC). *International Journal of Accounting and Financial Reporting* 5 (2): 133–143.

Transparency International 2020. Corruption Perceptions Index 2019. Retrieved from https://images.transparencycdn.org/images/2019_CPI_Report_EN_200331_141425.pdf. Accessed January 25, 2021.

Tri Vo. 2020. The Capital Flight from China: An Opportunity for Vietnam? *The International Affairs Review*. Retrieved from https://iar-gwu.org/blog/excrw7nyavz2dx1ueg9yw6wl5u2b5d. Accessed January 25, 2021.

UNCTAD. 2020. Global Foreign Direct Investment Projected to Plunge 40% in 2020. Retrieved from https://unctad.org/news/global-foreign-direct-investment-projected-plunge-40-2020#:~:text=Global%20foreign%20direct%20investment%20(FDI,UNCTAD's%20World%20Investment%20Report%202020.&text=In%20addition%2C%20FDI%20is%20projected,in%202022%2C%20the%20report%20says. Accessed January 25, 2021.

Van Nguyen, and Cao Nguyen. 2020. A Series of Businesses Fell into Losses, Negative Equity. Retrieved from https://laodong.vn/kinh-te/hang-loat-doanh-nghiep-roi-vao-canh-thua-lo-am-von-so-huu-846761.ldo. Accessed January 25, 2021.

World Bank. 2018. Enhancing Enterprise Competitiveness and SME Linkages World Bank. Paper presented at the AmCham Supplier Day 2018, HCMC.

World Bank. 2020. Doing Business 2020.

WEF. (2019). The Global Competitiveness Report 2019. Geneva: World Economic Forum.

Zhou, Cissy, and Finbarr Bermingham. 2019. Indonesia, Malaysia to Benefit with Vietnam Struggling to Cope with China Trade War Exodus. *South China Morning Post*, May 8.

CHAPTER 3

The Philippines: Decades Lost

Roderick Macdonald

Abstract By 1960, the Philippines had closed its borders to foreign ownership and thus all but eliminated foreign direct investment. It also curtailed imports and the terms of a transitory period of 'free trade' with the United States had left domestic firms incapable of competitive exports. The situation changed marginally in the 1990s under Ramos. Up to that time, the economy of the Philippines was stagnant. The Marcos administration had partially turned around the economy but ultimately failed due to excessive debt. Much of today's rapid growth is explained by business process outsourcing, that exports 30% of value added, and retailing. Foreign direct investment is permitted in both sectors, and retailing is aided on the demand side by personal remittances.

Keywords Closed economy · Ownership · Retail · Business process outsourcing · Remittances

Introduction: Closure, Opening and Performance of the Philippine Economy

The Philippines had a fast-growing economy before the onset of covid-19. Not only was it among the fastest growing in the region, it is among the fastest growing in the world as Table 3.1 reveals. If we exclude small

R. Macdonald, *Open and Closed Economies*,
https://doi.org/10.1007/978-3-030-79534-4_3

Table 3.1 Fastest growing economies worldwide, small countries excepted

Countries with population over 10 million			*Countries with population over 60 million*		
Rank		*Ratio 2018/2009*	*Rank*		*Ratio 2018/2009*
1	China	1.715666028	1	China	1.71566603
2	Ethiopia	1.670750842	2	Ethiopia	1.67075084
3	Myanmar	1.606807705	3	Bangladesh	1.5403071
4	Bangladesh	1.540307099	4	India	1.53690815
5	India	1.536908155	5	Vietnam	1.49062133
6	Cambodia	1.531026563	6	Philippines	1.4389248
7	Vietnam	1.490621325			
8	Georgia	1.464257363			
9	Uzbekistan	1.452315947			
10	Philippines	1.438924802			

Source Author's calculations based on World Bank national accounts data, and OECD National Accounts data files

populations such as the Virgin Islands, the Faroe Islands, the Channel Islands, Gibraltar, Liechtenstein and others, the Philippines are among the six consistently fastest growing economies in the world since 1995. It had the ninth highest rate of growth in GDP per capita from 2015 to 2019 among nations with a population over 10 million. Before the covid-19 pandemic, there were many arguments for projecting this growth into the years to come, such as the demographic sweet spot in which the Philippines is arriving (a large proportion of the population is of working age), and the prospects of the business process outsourcing industry (firms providing back office services, such as accounting or IT, and/or front office services such as marketing, sales and after-sales; these firms are an important source of growth for the Philippine economy).

This consistent, long-term, fast paced growth would make the Philippines a poster child for an open economy… except that the Philippines is far from an open economy.

The Philippine economy *has* been opening slowly and reluctantly since the 1990s. Trade has been increasing since 1985, but 1997 was the peak of trade as a percentage of GDP, dropping from 108 to 69% by 2019. Foreign ownership is heavily restricted, and trade policy has been markedly protectionist almost since the inception of the republic. Indeed, the Philippines have arguably attempted to close the economy since before independence. As for mobility of labour, expats need to obtain three different permits to work in the Philippines: (1) a work visa (the most common being the Pre-arranged Employment Visa or 9(G) visa), (2) an alien employment permit and (3) a provisional permit to work. The only claim that the Philippines have to an open economy is that remittances from Filipinos working abroad are equal to nearly 10% of GDP. Remittance are transfers of funds from persons working abroad to someone in the home country. Among countries with large populations, only the Ukraine and Egypt have recently surpassed the Philippines in personal remittance inflows.

The recent performance of the economy of the Philippines stands in stark contrast to the results of the last half of the twentieth century. Data are not easily available previous to 1960, and the Philippine economy began to open after the start of the Ramos administration in 1992 with effect delayed somewhat, so the comparison years chosen are 1960–1995. However, Fig. 3.1 shows the comparative sluggishness from 1950 using Penn World Table data. Table 3.2 shows that the Philippines had the second-worst performance among larger ASEAN nations over 1962–1995, barely besting Burma/Myanmar, with its terribly mismanaged economy that was also closed for some time. Incredibly, even war-torn and embargoed Vietnam performed better. These results are probably skewed by the artificial exchange rate of the Philippine peso after the Second World War. When the peso finally was allowed to float with respect to the US dollar in 1961, it dropped from 0.5 to 0.27 $US. However, even halving the starting GDP per capita would result in a lower growth rate than those enjoyed by neighbouring economies.

The following sections will first examine how the Philippines became a closed economy and then analyse the economic performance that resulted from that closure in greater detail. Finally, the current performance will be explained partly by a timid opening of the economy since the 1990s, and partly by some growth in GDP that is not an increase in the capacity to produce wealth—unless you blindly define wealth as GDP.

A Brief Overview of Philippine International Trade Before 1946

Although there was probably a small amount of trade between India and the Philippines, any Hindu and Buddhist influence probably arrived via relations with the Majapahit Empire (late thirteenth to early sixteenth centuries) centered in the Island of Java of present-day Indonesia. The

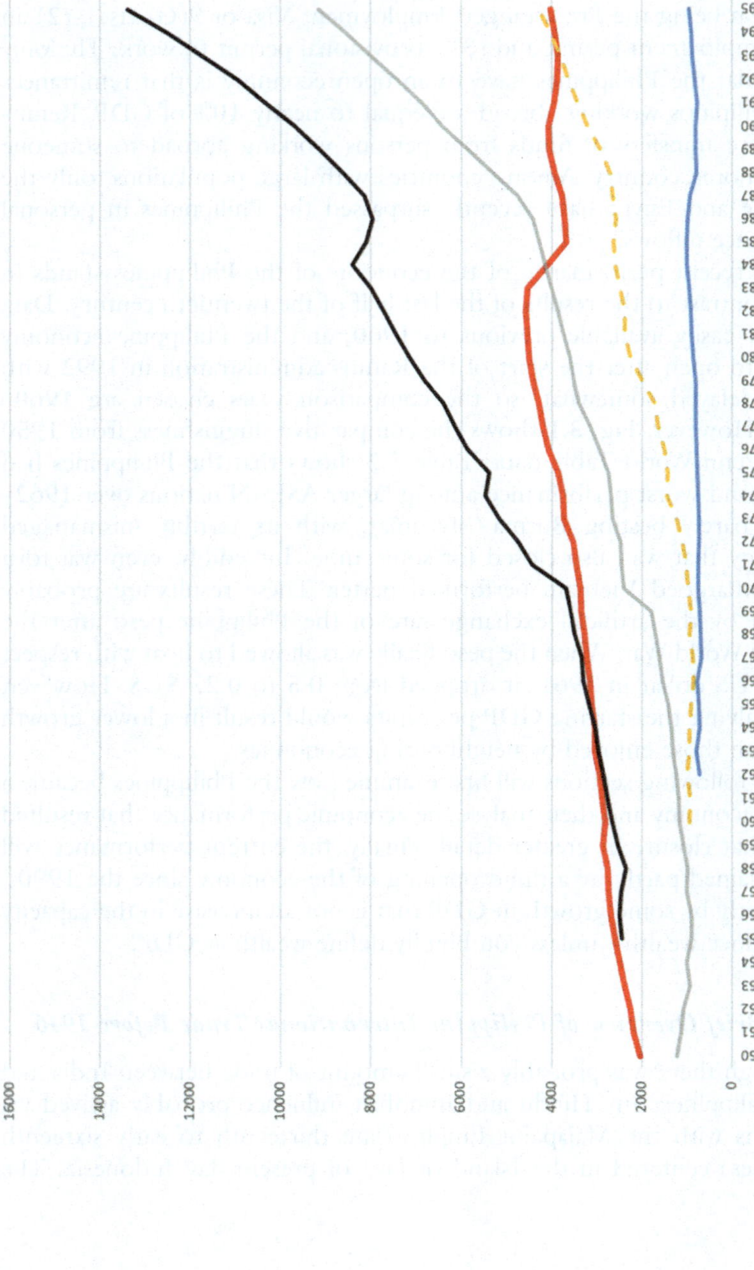

Fig. 3.1 GDP per capita compared 1960–1995. Using expenditure-side real GDP at chained PPPs (in million 2011US$) (*Data source* Author's calculations based on Penn World Table 9.1, Feenstra et al. [2015])

Table 3.2 Growth of larger ASEAN economies. Statistics report the relationship between GDP per capita in 1962 and 1995, with the exception of Vietnam. World Bank national accounts data, and OECD National Accounts data files

Country	*Ratio 1995/1962*	*CAGR 1962–1995 (%)*
Philippines	1.37	1
Malaysia	4.70	7
Thailand	7.36	9
Indonesia	4.25	6
Myanmar	1.32	1
Viet Nam (1970–1995)	2.07	3

Kawi script, in which the earliest dated document of the Philippines was written, came from Java.

Filipino merchants travelled to Guangzhou and Quanzhou (China) for trade at the end of the tenth century.

Traders from the Middle East brought Islam to Southeast Asia in the thirteenth century, and both Arabs and Malays had brought that religion to the Philippines (especially to the Sulu Islands, Mindanao, but also further north) in the fourteenth century.

Europeans arrived in 1521 when Magellan, a Portuguese navigator working for the Spanish crown, landed on the Eastern Samar Island of Homonhon. After 40 years of the usual pleasantries with the locals and with other European empire builders, Spain made the Philippines a colony. This led to new experiences of internationalism. There was mobility of 'labor' into the country in the form of fortune seekers who would constitute the top level of labelling by ethnic origin (*peninsulares*—from the Iberian peninsula, *insulares*—'pure' Spaniards born in the Philippine Islands, mestizos—mixed blood *de Español* or *de Sangley* [Chinese], *tornatras*, [Filipino, Spanish and Chinese ancestry] and then *indios*—Austronesian origin—and *negritos*—Aeta origin). Within Spain, the wealthy aristocracy was thriving on the riches of the Americas while trade and agriculture were shunned by the rest of the population. This created a situation where the majority looked for support by attaching themselves to rich nobles or the Church. (Moses 1893) This was seen as preferable to productive toil, but did not satisfy the more ambitious. Over the fifteenth and sixteenth centuries, the population of Spain declined from 10 to 6 million. The expulsion of the Jews and the Moriscos contributed to this, but it is also true that large numbers sought their fortune outside the country. Perhaps they brought this rent-seeking approach to business and the economy with them to the Philippines.

The Philippines also served as a sort of trading post or clearing house for Asia goods on their way to Europe or at least elsewhere in the Spanish Empire, particularly with the Manila-Acapulco trade referred to variously as Manila Galleons, *tornaviaje* and *Galyon ng Maynila at Acapulco*. Bjork (1998) argues that this trade made little sense for Spain, but fit well with Chinese and Mexican interests. This may well have been a first lesson in profit benefitting the few, and of international trade benefitting foreigners. In any case, a Spanish royal decree in 1804 ended the partial subsidy[1] that supported the arrangement, and the trade came to an end in 1815. By this time, however, industrialisation was leading to a wealthier Europe and demand both for raw materials (such as hemp) and for pleasant consumables such as sugar and tobacco. The proceeds from these exports allowed the landowners to purchase the products of European industrialisation, leading to a deeper experience of international trade beyond being a mere trading post. Not so with the tenant farmers, because their rents rose to 70% of the harvest and financing became extortionary in the nineteenth century (McCoy 2009).

The Spanish colony experience came to an end in 1898 with the extinction of the Spanish Empire. The Filipino elite had acquired notions of freedom and independence in the nineteenth century, leading to various resistance movements. The Spanish American War led the US to support these movements until victory over Spain made the Philippines a US colony. Being labelled a coloniser did not sit well with politicians in the United States of America. The solution was to shift the Philippines from military to civil administration, erecting bicameral government institutions in the Philippines with elected representatives (the US Congress Organic Act in 1907 and the Jones Law in 1916—the Philippine Commission being an appointed body in 1907).

The civil administration oversaw considerable improvement in ports, roads, railways, communications and even the financial system. There was an attempt to reform the agricultural system by transferring land to farm workers who had been virtually peasants, but it failed in the face of landowner resistance, in stark contrast to the experiences of Korea and Taiwan. Basic education also flourished, boosting literacy and providing some basis for social mobility and some real democracy.

In the 1930s, political forces within the United States and within the Philippines wrangled over the terms of an eventual Philippine independence, leading to the 1934 Philippine Independence Act (called the Tydings–McDuffie Act) establishing a procedure for the Philippines to acquire independence after a ten-year transition. It was thus in the years of the Great Depression that the first seeds of Philippine economic policy were planted (see Sicat 2008, 4). This time, the experience of European colonisation (as well as later terms of independence[2] imposed by some parties in the U.S.) explain much of the protectionist tone of Philippine economic policy in the twentieth century. The National Economic Protectionism Association, founded in 1934, still exists today.

Independence, Original Sin and Barriers to Trade

Japanese occupation during World War II slightly delayed the independence plan. The liberation of the Philippines in September 1945 saw between 100,000 and 300,000 civilians die in Manila alone and much of the country's infrastructure destroyed. One million Filipinos died in the reconquest of the islands. Japan lost and is blamed for these deaths. Perhaps rightly so. There was a brief continuation of the Commonwealth status until July 4, 1946. Perhaps Americans chose this date—it was not until the 1960s that the Philippine Independence Day was changed to June 12.

The US provided funds to rebuild the Philippines (estimates vary from $US520 million to 2 billion; the most detailed account is Sicat 2019), and made good on the plan for an independent Philippines. However, there were strings attached. Free trade (with quotas imposed on key Philippine exports) with the United States was to be at an imposed exchange rate that hamstrung exporters in the Philippines. The pre-war exchange rate, from a time when the Philippine industrial base and the infrastructure had not yet been destroyed, was the rate dictated by the United States. The Maddison data (Bolt et al. 2018) estimate that the GDP per capita of the Philippines in 1946 was less than half the 1940 level, which was not attained again until 1962. US GDP per capita, in contrast, had increased 12% from 1941 to 1946. The slanted playing field for 'free trade' with the US would ultimately reinforce the protectionist vision and dislike of foreign ownership that began to appear in the 1930s, and do so at a time when most of the developed world was moving from protectionism to gradual globalisation. Chikiamco (2020) called the gross over-evaluation of the peso the 'original sin' of the Philippines.[3] The experience would lead to the creation of the Tariff Commission in 1953, and decades of tariffs and non-tariff measures.

The 1970s saw some softening in this resistance to trade. In 1973 the Marcos martial law administration established the National Economic and Development Authority, foreseen in the constitution of that same year, absorbing the National Economic Development Authority which had previously replaced the National Economic Council of 1935. It oversaw the Tariff Commission. Executive Order No. 230 would reorganise the National Economic and Development Authority in 1987.

Meanwhile, the Philippines acceded to the General Agreement on Tariffs and Trades in December 27, 1979 and would be included in the World Trade Organisation upon its creation on January 1, 1995.

The mandate and functions of the Tariff commission were redefined by Republic Act No. 10863, the Customs Modernisation and Tariff Act in 2016.

These series of dates reveal influences within (various presidential administrations) and without (what was eventually correctly or incorrectly called the Washington consensus) encouraging the Philippines to open up to international trade. These influences have had modest success. There is some improvement in policy. The Philippines continue to use tariffs to protect local producers so that imported manufactured goods competing with locally produced goods face higher tariffs than those without local competition. The country has set ceilings for 67% of its tariff lines (products as defined in lists of tariff rate) in the World Trade Organisation (WTO), with a simple average WTO bound tariff rate of 25.7%.[4] Figure 3.2 shows that, as of 2017, the Philippines had middling levels of trade barriers in the form of tariffs. The list of tariffs (ranking 44th in the out of 140 nations in the World Competitiveness Index[5]) and non-tariff measures (42 out of 140), even within the ASEAN free trade zone[6] is an improvement upon the past.

Unfortunately, the trade performance of the country has followed a generally diminishing trend with a fairly constant negative trade balance (see Fig. 3.3 Comparative trade (% of GDP)). The Philippines are internationally reputed for the quality of seafarers, nurses and domestic workers, but not for products nor exported services (other than low-end business process such as call centers in the twenty-first century). Even today, although about 75% of gross exports are domestic value

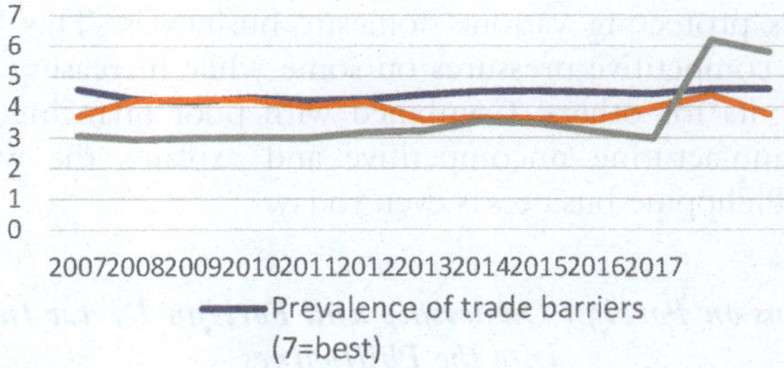

Fig. 3.2 Philippine barriers to trade 2007–2019 (*Data sources* WEF [2017, 2019])

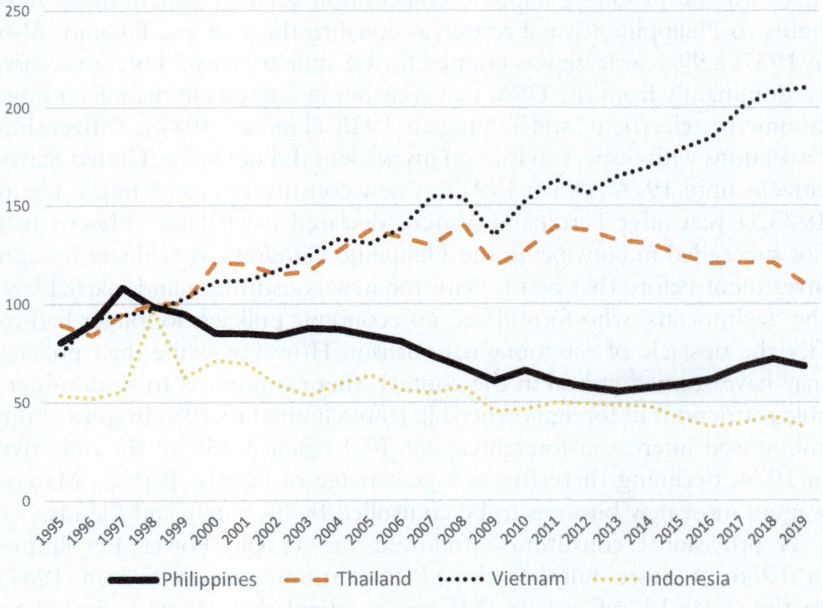

Fig. 3.3 Comparative trade as % GDP (*Data source* World Bank national accounts data, and OECD National Accounts data files)

added, much of this domestic value added is accounted for by agriculture, fishing and mining. Imports are depressed by the purchasing power of the population, the highly negative trade balance, and remaining trade barriers protecting various domestic businesses. This last protection reduces competitive pressures on some while increasing the cost of imported inputs for others. Combined with poor financing, this keeps domestic manufacturing uncompetitive and explains the weak export potential of Philippine businesses even today.

Restrictions on Foreign Ownership and Foreign Direct Investment into the Philippines

Article 12 of the 1935 Constitution of the Philippines had restricted ownership of real or business assets to Filipinos or entities with a maximum 40% foreign ownership. However, the 1947 'Parity Amendment' of the (1935) Philippine constitution granted American citizens rights to Philippine natural resources equal to those of any Filipino. Also in 1947, a 99-year lease was granted for US military bases. Foreign actors, predominantly from the USA, had controlling interests in manufacturing, commerce, electricity and mining in 1948 (Lindsey 1987). Citizenship restrictions with respect to foreign investment did not affect United States citizens until 1974 (Dolan 1991). A new constitution came into force in 1973, a year after Ferdinand Marcos declared martial law. Marcos had not succeeded in convincing the Philippine Congress to facilitate foreign investment before that point. With the new constitution and martial law, the 'technocrats' who formulated his economic policies no longer had to face the obstacle of economic nationalism. However, while their policies may have seemed radical in the context, there continued to be considerable restrictions in foreign ownership (often limited to 40%) in spite of the announced interest in foreign capital. FDI reached 35% of the objective in 1974, declining thereafter as a percentage of targets. Perhaps Marcos wanted most new business to be controlled by his family and friends.

A provisional constitution followed the People Power Revolution in 1986. A more fully developed constitution was ratified in 1987. Sections 10–12 of article XII are particularly relevant, excluding foreigners from professions and limiting foreign ownership 'in certain industries' to 40%.[7] In practice, approval by the Philippine Board of Investment was required for any new majority business ownership.

In summary, foreign ownership has been severely restricted in the Philippines since independence with the sole and resented exception of American interests that ended in 1974. The impact of the Marcos regime was minimal, especially because the ending of American privilege counterbalanced any search for other foreign capital.

Economic Results

Figure 3.4, 1995, presents the variations in wealth of the Philippines for the comparison years of 1960–1995. It appears to indicate modest growth. Figure 3.5 qualifies this impression. Compared to Singapore and even to Malaysia, the Philippine economy seemed to be almost standing still. This is perhaps somewhat of an exaggeration. There was definite improvement for a small percentage of citizens, and many left the countryside to seek their fortune in the big city. Unfortunately, many of these found their destiny in slums. And, if many left the countryside, others remained. Filipino farmers and fishermen were desperately poor in the twentieth century, to a great extent because their markets were inefficient and controlled by a wealthy few and in part because many in farming were crop workers who did not own any land, while others had unclear rights over their family property. Data on wealth distribution from that epoch is sparse, but probably would indicate a similar or worse situation to recent data discussed below. Figure 3.1 above gave some idea of how the buying power of the average Filipino compared to that of citizens in other countries.

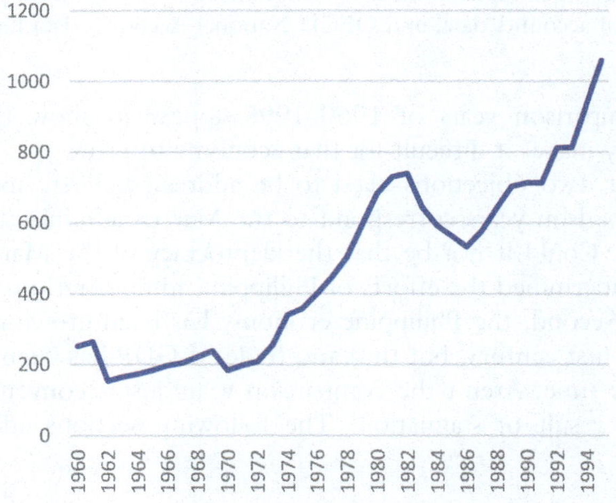

Fig. 3.4 Philippine GDP per capita 1960–1995 (*Data source* World Bank national accounts data, and OECD National Accounts data files)

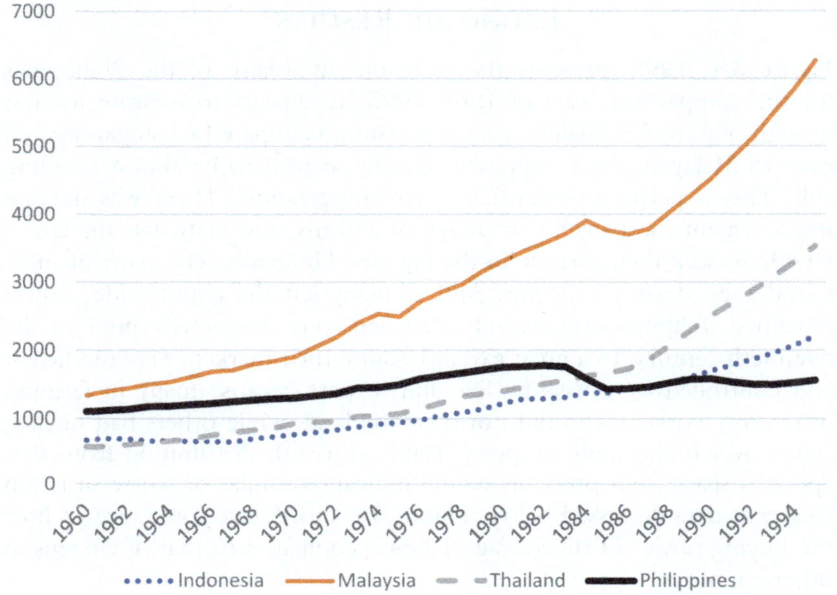

Fig. 3.5 GDP per capita compared (constant 2010 US$) (*Data source* World Bank national accounts data, and OECD National Accounts data files)

The comparison years of 1960–1995 appear to show that closing an economy makes it difficult for that economy to grow.

However, two objections need to be addressed. First, about half of those comparison years correspond to the Marcos administration in the Philippines. Could it not be that the kleptocracy of the Marcos administration undermined the efforts of Philippine administrations before and after him? Second, the Philippine economy has been growing rapidly in the twenty-first century, but the ratio trade-to-GDP has been decreasing at the same time. Aren't the comparison years just a convenient choice to get the result of stagnation? The following sections address these objections.

A Closer Look at the Marcos Regime

It is important to understand that the Marcos regime (1965–1986), although it accounts for more than half the 35 comparison years, is not the root cause of the economic woes of the Philippines in the second half of the twentieth century.

Data for the early post war years is incomplete and so is excluded from the comparison years, but a reasonably indicative description can be drawn from what is available. To support a sense of patriotism and as part of efforts to minimise foreign participation in the economy, a succession of governments during the 1950s and 1960s focused on import substitution that saw the rise of exclusivist economic nationalism. Over 1949 and 1950, imports fell by almost 40% to US$342 million and surpassed the 1949 level in only one year during the 1950s.

At first net, domestic product from manufacturing grew rapidly, averaging 12% growth per annum in real terms during the first half of the 1950s, contributing to an average 7.7% growth in the GNP, a higher rate than in any subsequent five-year period. However, in the second half of the 1950s, the growth rate of manufacturing fell by about a third to an average of 7.7%, and real GNP growth was down to 4.9%. It should be remembered that much of Philippine manufacturing was destroyed or damaged during the Japanese occupation and the American re-taking of the Philippine Island, particularly in Luzon. The Philippines were simply getting back to pre-war productive capacity, but with the handicap of unfair competition from American imports with their exchange rate advantage.

In addition, prior to 1970, Philippine exports consisted mainly of agricultural or mineral products in raw or minimally processed form. From 1960 to early 1962, import controls were phased out. Imports increased rapidly. Another acceleration of imports occurred in the early 1970s, this time raising the import to GNP ratio to around 25%, the level at which it remained into the 1990s. The Philippines had difficulty in generating sufficient exports to pay for its imports. In the forty years from 1950 through 1990, the trade balance was positive in only two years: 1963 and 1973.

In the 1970s, the country began to export manufactured products, especially garments and electronic components, and the prices of some traditional exports declined. By 1988 non-traditional exports comprised 75% of the total value of goods shipped abroad. However, total exports did not take off until the 1990s.

The 1970s (years of the Marcos administration) return exceptional results against the general trend of the post war twentieth century as witnessed by Fig. 3.5. There is strong growth for a little over a decade.

There is a slight decline in the late 1960s when Marcos first took power, and a strong decline from 1982 until 1986 as opposition to the regime heated up.

That administration made two major changes in economic policy: (1) a large fraction of business ownership was transferred to the government (controlled by Marcos), as well as to the Marcos family and friends; and (2) the central government borrowed heavily in order to expand the industrial base of the Philippines. Of course, the two changes are not unrelated, as the new funds were used to the benefit of both government-controlled and crony businesses. Marcos has been strongly demonised for these two economic changes, as well as for his authoritarian regime that was far from benign. However, both economic changes should be understood in context.

Marcos moved control of the Philippine economy from the hands of the leading families into his own hands, those of his cronies and to the direct ownership of the government that he controlled. This is one of the reasons he is labelled a kleptocrat. It is nonetheless true that an inordinate portion of the Philippine economy was in the hands of a few families before the time of Marcos, and after the time of Marcos until today.[8] These family holdings are generally in businesses that do not produce internationally tradeable goods, nor use imports as input. The families had an influence on economic policy before and after the Marcos administration, fostering the economic nationalism born in the 1930s. Again, this was also quite understandable given the unhappy experience of free trade with the United States immediately following World War II.

Marcos also borrowed heavily in the 1970s with an intent to stimulate the industry sector (perhaps with particular emphasis on the holdings of government, his family and his cronies). External debt increased from US$722 million in 1965 to US$12 billion in 1980 (Erbe 1982). The recourse to debt was an obvious mistake from the hindsight of the late 1980s and the 1990s after Paul Volker raised US interest rates to 20% in a successful effort to stave off American stagflation caused by Richard Nixon's economic decisions of 1971. This made the Marcos borrowing extremely burdensome.

The recourse to debt rather than FDI was in part motivated by economic nationalism (born in the 1930s and reinforced by the 'free trade' experience with the United States) and in part because Ferdinand Marcos wanted to control most new business either directly or through cronies. This recourse to debt contrasted with neighbouring countries

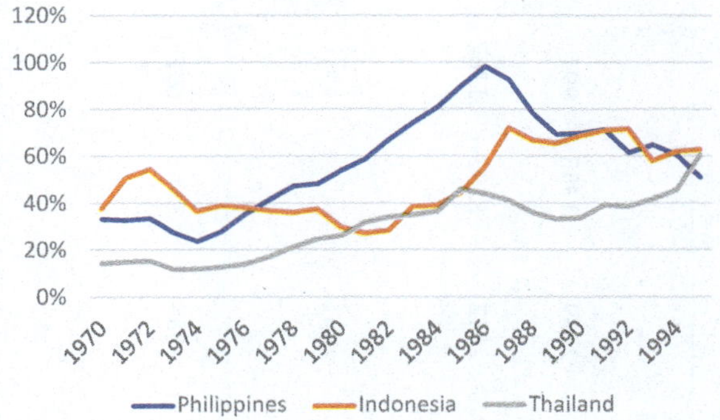

Fig. 3.6 External debt compared (*Data source* World Bank, International Debt Statistics)

(see Fig. 3.6) and would boomerang to a finance-draining effect during the high interest years of the 1980s. Today Ferdinand Marcos stands accused of saddling the Philippines with inordinate debt. However, absent Marcos, the other reigning families would have needed to do the same, or else the Philippines would not have experienced their growth spurt through to 1983. The country was short of capital.

Much is made of the Philippines being the richest country in South-east Asia in 1950 (and a few erroneously assert that Singapore was the poorest). Three considerations reveal that this myth is fallacious. First, the data we do have (See Table 3.3) clearly indicate that the British territories of Hong Kong, Malaysia and Singapore, as well as Japan and Taiwan, were all wealthier than the Philippines, with Korea not too far behind. Second, the estimates we have are based on the conversion of local currencies following the 1944 Bretton Woods arrangement, with the Philippine peso tied to an unreasonable exchange rate, overestimating Philippine wealth in US dollars. Third, the Philippines were ravaged by the Second World War. Most of the Pacific archipelago nations received funding from the United States of America (Indonesia ($215 million), Taiwan ($1.051 billion) and Japan ($2.44 billion). These funding levels reflected the level of destruction in each country. The US did provide $US 800 billion in post war aid after destroying much of the industrial base in an effort to oust Japan from the Philippines. Unfortunately, due to quirks of how democratic government decisions are made in the USA,[9] the Bell Trade Act of 1946 and the 'free trade' years that followed erased much of the impact of these funds

Table 3.3 Comparative wealth after World War II

	Cambodia	*Hong Kong*	*Indonesia*	*Japan*	*Republic of Korea*	*Malaysia*	*Philippines*	*Singapore*	*Taiwan*	*Thailand*
Maddison's real GDP per capita in $US 2011, 1946				1903			791			
Maddison's real GDP per capita in $US 2011, 1950	553	4013	1175	2519	1122	2667	1310	2439	1355	991
PWT expenditure-based real GDP per capita $US 2011, 1965		5934	920	7966	1322	2940	2019	2642	3293	1367
World development Indicators, GDP per capita $US2010, 1960			690	8608	932	1354	1100	3503		571
World development Indicators, GDP per capita $US2010, 1965		4905	666	12,595	1156	1617	1206	4088		695

Note that the figures for the Philippines are probably based on the unrealistic exchange rate imposed by the Bell Trade Act. Also, the Chinese civil war led to the island of Formosa being settled by the nationalist side in 1949, so that economy was weakened in 1950

Sources Maddison Project Database, version 2018, Penn World Table, version 9.1 (Bolt et al. 2018), World bank World Development Indicators, author's calculations

in the Philippines. As a result, the Philippines were strapped for capital right up until the time of Marcos.

The 1970s resembled the 2020 US money market, although for different reasons. Interest rates were low because oil-producing nations needed to lend money. At the same time, there was a strong need for money in the Philippines. Just as in 2020 many in North America borrowed at low rates and increased their wealth with the boom of the stock market after the stimulus offered by the Trump administration, so too the Marcos administration sought to benefit from and harness the abundant cheap money available at the time. The result was the industrial boom indicated by Fig. 3.7 by manifesting the portion of GDP contributed by industry as opposed to services, agriculture, fisheries and forests.

Unfortunately, a portion of the incoming funds were diverted to the enrichment of the crony club. Further, funds directed to one potentially game-changing project were mismanaged by both the Marcos and the Aquino administration that followed his fall: nuclear power.[10]

Although protection may have made Philippine manufacture uncompetitive, it is also true that the prohibitive cost of energy also was a factor. Initiated under Marcos, the two-reactor nuclear power plant project in Bataan would provide cheaper electricity to all of Luzon, where about half the Philippine population and industry resides. However, corruption affected both the original contract (awarded to Westinghouse rather than General Electric) and subsequent use of funds. The General Electric bid was two power plants for US$700 million. The Westinghouse

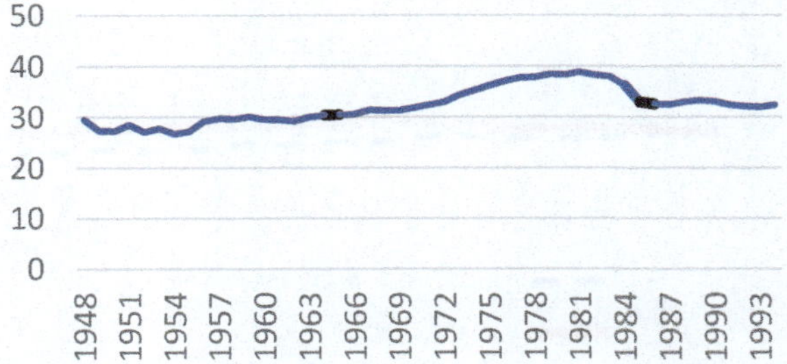

Fig. 3.7 Industry contribution to GDP (*Data sources* Author's calculation from PSA [2020a])

bid was for one plant with two reactors for US$500 million, that eventually became one reactor for US$1.1 billion, then, after additional safety features added, US$2.2 billion. The Philippine government borrowed and committed to expenditures and the plant was built, but never saw operations because the Aquino administration shut down the project (see Mendoza et al. (2016b) for a fairly complete analysis and timeline of the project from context to closure.) As a result, the Philippines took on all the risk of a massive investment, then walked away from any possible returns, and Philippine businesses and consumers alike remain saddled with high electricity costs today.

The vaguely S-shaped curve of GDP and GDP per capita growth for the Philippines during the Marcos years and their aftermath is the manifestation of a re-organisation of ownership and with it, a change of emphasis to manufacture under Marcos and back to services after him, as Fig. 3.8 indicates. Thus, domestic manufacturing was crushed in the early years of independence, then overly protected for a few years, nurtured but also controlled by Marcos, then neglected after the People Power revolution as the oligarchic families organised economic policy around their businesses: non-exportable goods and services.

As a result, the Marcos regime does present an anomaly in the evolution of the Philippine economy, but neither explains the stagnation of that economy in the last half of the twentieth century, nor is allowed to overcome that stagnation. Rather, it reveals how economic policy before and after the regime is responsible from much of that stagnation, providing rent-seeking conditions for business interests centered on non-tradeable goods.

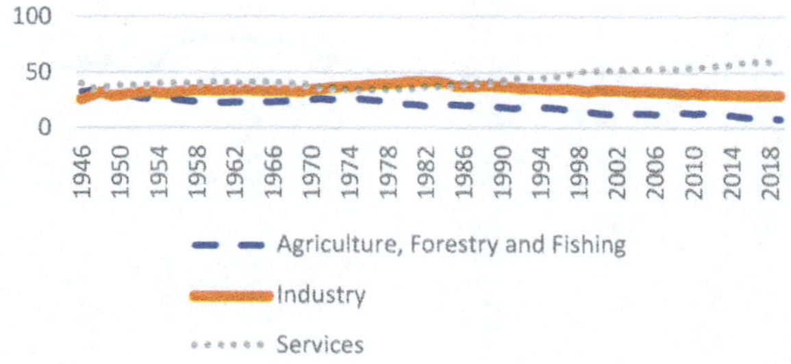

Fig. 3.8 Evolving GDP structure at constant 2018 prices. Vertical axis in percent (*Data source* PSA [2020b])

The Philippine Economy Since the 1990s

The second objection to a link between closure of the Philippine economy and stagnation is the fact that recent rapid growth coincides with a decrease in the trade to GDP ratio.

The Fidel Ramos administration came into power on June 30, 1992 and would prove to be a (modest) turning point for the economy of the Philippines. Change in fact began a year earlier, on June 13, 1991.

De Iure Opening to Foreign Capital

A country can establish a policy that allows foreign ownership and thus encourages foreign capital to enter the country. That is the law, ***de iure***. This does not mean that funds will in fact enter, de facto. If there is no interesting investment opportunity, funds will not enter.

The Foreign Investments Act of 1991 (or Republic Act No. 7042 (as amended by Republic Act No. 8179) sought to increase foreign direct investment by loosening the restrictions. It did so by allowing foreign direct investment with 100% ownership except in certain cases. The intent was to invite foreign direct investment where it could benefit the Philippine economy—large investors in exporting industries; smaller operations with advanced technologies and generally not threatening established domestic rivals. This translated into three lists: (A) activities reserved to Philippine nationals by the Philippine Constitution and specific laws—foreign ownership was limited to zero or various minority levels; (B) activities where, for reasons of national security, health, morals and protection of small- and medium-scale enterprises, foreign ownership is limited to 40% in some activities; (C) areas of investment in which existing enterprises already serve adequately the needs of the economy and the consumer and do not require further foreign investments. These Foreign Investment Negative Lists have been modified ten times as of 2020. Although restrictive and a little complicated, this development provided two advances for the foreign investor. First, the entire optic changed to restrictions being the exception rather than the almost universal case with exceptions. This is true even if the number of exceptions seems more numerous than the activities covered by the general permission of foreign majority ownership. The second advantage is a corollary. The potential foreign investor need only consult the lists to verify if majority ownership is excluded before proceeding to more detailed analysis.

The Special Economic Zone Act of 1995 (Republic Act No. 7916, amended by Republic Act 8748) provided for the establishment of special economic zones. Today there are numerous (over 300) export processing zones, free trade zones and certain industrial estates that are all associated with special tax treatment and allow importation of goods free of customs duties. Although the Act did not diminish restrictions on foreign ownership, it built upon the 1991 Foreign Investments Act by making investments in those zones more attractive. In 2000, the Board of the Philippines Economic Zone Authority (PEZA) established guidelines on the registration of IT Enterprises and IT Parks and Buildings and offered various incentives for the establishment of IT businesses. A 2017 resolution of the Board of PEZA extended the definition of economic zones to include the land on which 'IT buildings' are located.

Republic Act 8762, known as the Retail Trade Liberalisation Act of 2000, allowed foreign ownership of retailers of luxury goods if the paid-up capital was over US$250,000, and any retailer with paid-up capital of US$7,500,000 or more (provided individual stores had US$830,000 capital investments). A 2021 amendment saw this minimum lowered to US$1,000,000.

De Facto Inward Movement of Capital

Figure 3.9 presents the FDI performance of the Philippines since 1970. Two characteristics are obvious: saw-toothed variations until 2010 and a dramatic change since 2010. The saw-toothed variations from the 1991

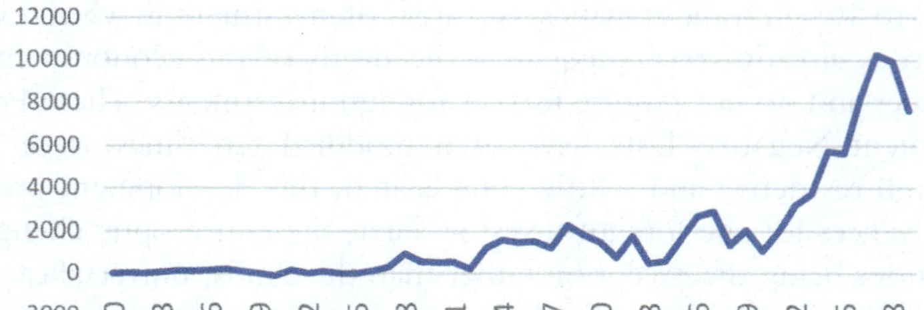

Fig. 3.9 Foreign direct investment, net inflows (BoP, million current US$) 1970–2019 (*Data sources* International Monetary Fund, Balance of Payments database, supplemented by data from the United Nations Conference on Trade and Development and official national sources)

Foreign Investment Act up to 2010 are explained in large part by the Asian financial crisis of 1997–1998 and the global financial crisis of 2007–2010. The upswing in 2010 occurs with the change of presidential regime from Gloria Macapagal-Arroyo (2001–2010) to Benigno S. Aquino III. Although the former regime boasted a superficial improvement in economic performance with 5% economic growth, it was marked by increasing poverty rates and various scandals leading to impeachment complaints in four different years. Similar observations can be made of the 1991–2001 period. The crises and regime changes overwhelmed any effect of changes in foreign ownership policy excepting, as we shall see below, foreign direct investment in retailing.

Figure 3.10 maintains the saw-tooth performance and link to financial crises and presidential regimes. In addition, it underlines the weakness of the Philippine performance compared to peers in the region. Singapore is notable absent from the figure. Singapore's lowest statistic over 1991–2018 is 4% of GDP in 1992, with most years varying from 15 to 20%. For the cumulative effect, see Fig. 3.11.

Policy, law and regulations not been the only impediment to foreign capital. Weak infrastructure in a sprawling and mountainous archipelago

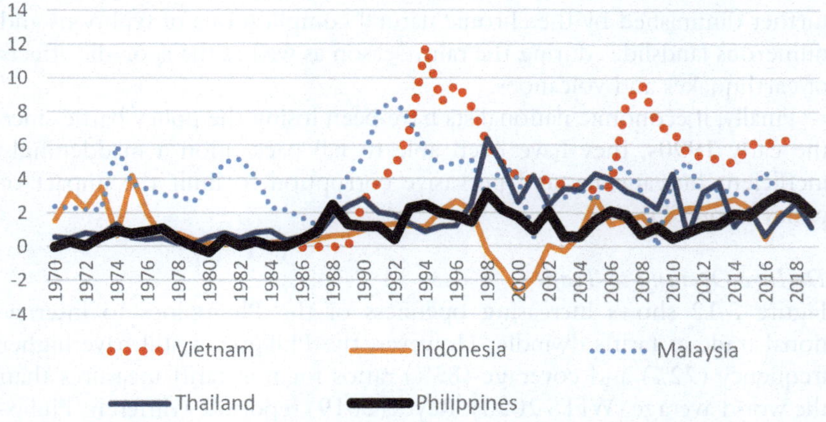

Fig. 3.10 Foreign direct investment inflows as % GDP for large ASEAN nations (*Data sources* International Monetary Fund, International Financial Statistics and Balance of Payments databases, World Bank, International Debt Statistics, and World Bank and OECD GDP estimates)

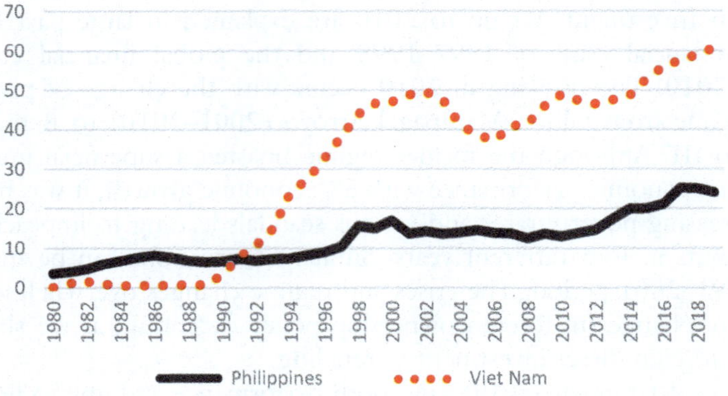

Fig. 3.11 Inward stock of FDI compared for Philippines and Vietnam (*Data source* UNCTADstat)

increases the cost of doing business. The Philippines are in dire need of massive infrastructure investments (ranking 63rd on World Bank Logistics Performance index, compared to 42nd for Vietnam and 35th for Thailand, see LPI [2020]) to deal with the numerous islands and extensive mountainous terrain. The effectiveness of the infrastructure in place is further diminished by the chronic natural complications of typhoons and numerous landslides during the rainy season as well as the sporadic effects of earthquakes and volcanoes.

Finally, if economic nationalists have been losing the policy battle since the early 1990s, they have been able to fall back upon a maddeningly inefficient bureaucracy and pervasive corruption to limit the impact of policy upon FDI.

De Iure Opening to Trade

Figure 3.12 shows increasing openness of the Philippines to international trade as tariffs dwindle. However, the Philippines still have higher frequency (72%) and coverage (85%) ratios for non-tariff measures than the world average (WITS 2020). Reyes (2019) reports 29 different Philippine agencies issuing non-tariff measures, with increases in the number of measures, the number of products covered and the number of product regulations from 2015 to 2018. Table 3.4 reveals the sluggishness with which trade opened, since all the pending partners have signed more agreements and more rapidly than the Philippines.

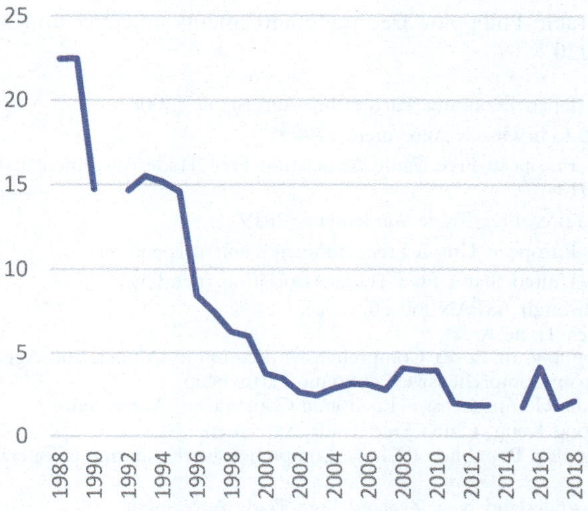

Fig. 3.12 Weighted mean of tariff applied to all products (*Data source* World Bank staff estimates using the World Integrated Trade Solution system, based on data from United Nations Conference on Trade and Development's Trade Analysis and Information System [TRAINS] database and the World Trade Organisation's [WTO] Integrated Data Base [IDB] and Consolidated Tariff Schedules [CTS] database)

De facto Opening to Trade

The Philippine economy has been opening to international trade since the 1990s, but very timidly. Figures 3.13, 3.14 and 3.15 tell a grim story: Philippine businesses were unable to compete in the export market. The major exception was business process outsourcing. It is studied below in the next section which examines the quality of GDP growth.

An Analysis of GDP Growth

The Production Approach

The five fastest growing sub-sectors of the Philippine economy from 2000 to 2019 were Professional and business services, Information and communication, Financial and insurance activities, Construction, ['other services', which we shall not consider] and Accommodation and Food services. Although construction can be cyclical in many advanced

Table 3.4 Table Philippine free trade agreements, effective and pending as of December 2020

- Philippines–Japan Economic Partnership Agreement (2008)
- ASEAN Trade in Goods Agreement (2009)
- Philippines–European Free Trade Association Free Trade Agreement (2016 effective 2018)
- Philippine–Korea Free Trade Agreement (2019)
- Philippines–European Union Free Trade Agreement (pending)
- Philippines–United States Free Trade Association (pending)

Agreements through ASEAN (all effective):

- ASEAN Free Trade Area
- ASEAN-Republic of Korea Comprehensive Economic Cooperation Agreement
- ASEAN-Japan Comprehensive Economic Partnership
- ASEAN-India Comprehensive Economic Cooperation Agreement
- ASEAN-Hong Kong, China Free Trade Agreement
- ASEAN-People's Republic of China Comprehensive Economic Cooperation Agreement
- ASEAN-Australia and New Zealand Free Trade Agreement

Sources Asia Regional Integration Center of the Asia Development Bank, Republic of the Philippines Tariff Commission, Republic of the Philippines Department of Trade and Industry

economies, in the Philippines it has grown every year since 2000. The following paragraphs examine some of these categories as available data permit.

Both of the fastest growing categories are part of an often-touted category for which hard to compare statistics are also available: IT-BPM or Information technology and business process management. Professional and business services have grown eight-fold; Information and communication have grown five-and-a-half-fold. IT-BPM grew 16% from 2016 to 2017, reaching 567 trillion (thousand million) pesos (PSA 2020c) in 2017. The image that most people have of this industry is of success in exploiting Filipino deference and Filipino mastery of English (more people speaking English than in Australia, Canada and New Zealand combined), to provide customer service. However, this is not quite accurate. Voice-based service (such as inbound and outbound call centers) is the largest employer with two-thirds of jobs within the IT-BPM category, and generates a little more than one half of the income. Computer programming, sales and marketing and computer consultancy and facilities management together combine for a third of income. Again, only one-third of the income is generated by transactions outside of the

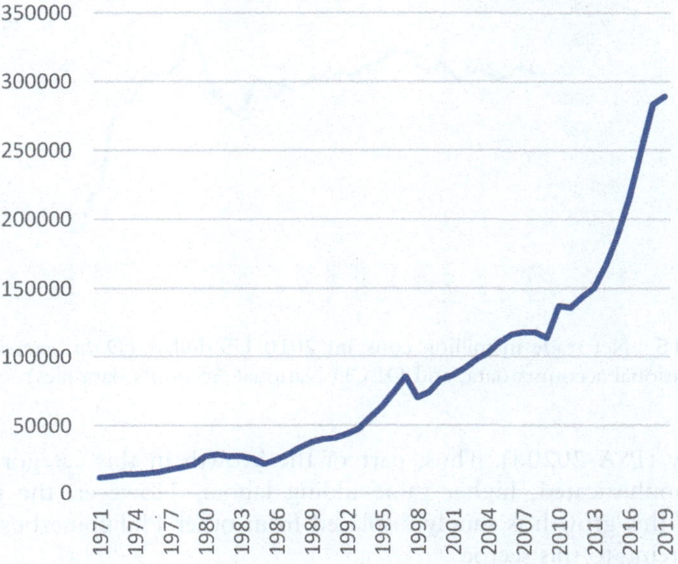

Fig. 3.13 Total trade in million constant 2010 US$ (*Data sources* World Bank national accounts data, and OECD National Accounts data files)

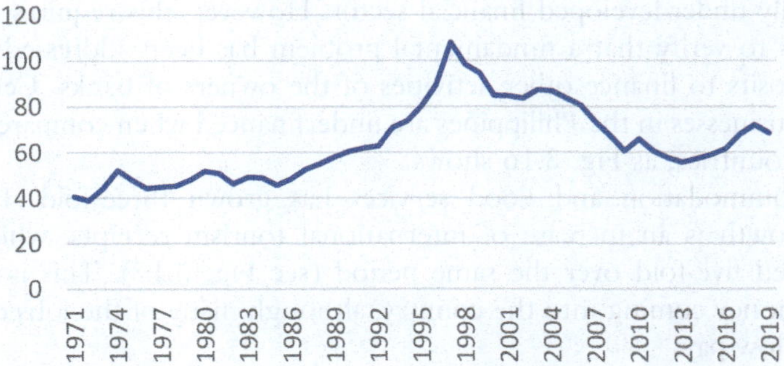

Fig. 3.14 Trade as a percentage of GDP (*Data sources* World Bank national accounts data, and OECD National Accounts data files)

Fig. 3.15 Net trade in million constant 2010 US dollars (*Data sources* World Bank national accounts data, and OECD National Accounts data files)

country (PSA 2020d). Thus, part of the growth in this category is in more sophisticated, higher value-adding labour. However, the greater part of this growth is simply displaced from other Philippine businesses outsourcing to this sector.

Financial and insurance services are the next fastest growing category. This is potentially crucial for the development of a Philippine economy that has been marked by insufficient credit for private enterprise and generally underdeveloped financial sector. However, this requires deeper analysis to verify that a fundamental problem has been addressed: using all deposits to finance other activities of the owners of banks. Certainly, most businesses in the Philippines are underfinanced when compared with other countries, as Fig. 3.16 shows.

Accommodation and Food services has grown three-fold. Part of this growth is an increase of international tourism receipts, which has increased five-fold over the same period (see Fig. 3.17). This is clearly fresh money coming into the country, although many of the jobs created have a low pay.

Many of the jobs in these fastest growing categories in the economy of the Philippines are skilled and high value added. Unfortunately, they are not the most important contributors to the growth rate of the Philippine economy. Size is also important. One percent change in an industry that is 5% of the economy has a greater impact than twenty percent change in an industry that is 0.01% of the economy.

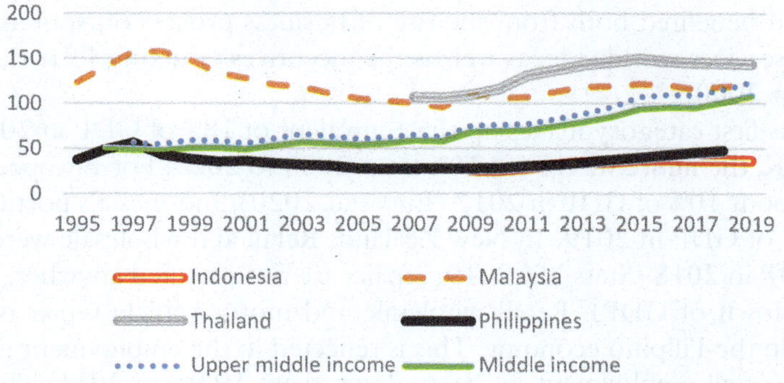

Fig. 3.16 Domestic credit to private sector compared (*Data sources* International Monetary Fund, International Financial Statistics and data files, and World Bank and OECD GDP estimates)

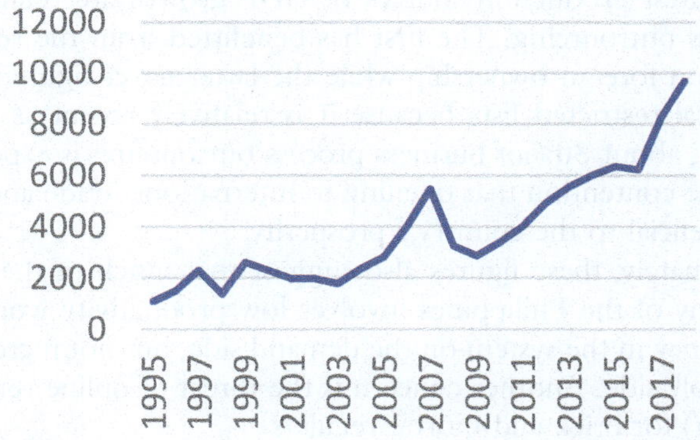

Fig. 3.17 International tourism, receipts in million current US dollars (*Data sources* World Tourism Organisation, Yearbook of Tourism Statistics, Compendium of Tourism Statistics and data files)

The five categories that contributed to the largest change in value from 2000 to 2019 were Wholesale and retail trade and repair of motor vehicles and motorcycles, Manufacturing, Financial and insurance activities, Construction, Professional and business services. Of these, the first two (trade and manufacturing) are almost double the size of the others. The first category benefited from the Retail Trade Liberalisation Act of 2000, while the last (professional and business services) was never on a restricted list and benefited both from the rise of business process outsourcing and of IT services worldwide, as well as the incentives targeting IT parks from at least 2000.

This first category makes up the equivalent of 18% of GDP in 2019. In the UK, the figure was about 10% from 2000 to 2020. For Europe, it was also about 10% of GDP in 2017 (Eurostat 2020). Indonesia's portion was 12.8% of GDP in 2019. In New Zealand, Retail and wholesale were 9.3% of GDP in 2018 (Stats NZ 2019; repairs are not specified anywhere in the breakdown of GDP). Retail wholesale and motor vehicle repair is oversized in the Filipino economy. This is reflected in the employment figures: 18.7% of all employment in 2014, down from 19.9% in 2011. The only category of services with greater employment in 2014 was 'Community, Social & Personal Services' at 22% of all jobs. Within the former category, somewhere between 50 and 75% (or between 10 and 15% of all jobs in the Philippines) are in retail establishments.

The greatest production sources of GDP growth are retail and business process outsourcing. The first has benefitted from the relaxation of restriction on foreign ownership while the latter never figured on any of the historical restricted lists because it is relatively recent as a business. In addition, about 30% of business process outsourcing is exported. This supports the contention that opening to international trade and financing can be beneficial to the country's prosperity.

Unfortunately, these figures also suggest that much of the growth in the economy of the Philippines involves low productivity work.[11] There is some money in the system on the demand side, but not increasing skills on the supply side. Another concern is the threat of online retailing (and wholesaling) for brick-and-mortar retailers.

Financial and insurance activities constitute the category that was the next largest contributor to GDP growth. Jobs in these activities grew from 0.83% of all employment in 1992 to 1.34% in 2020 (see Fig. 3.18). These are considered mostly high skill, high value activities, auguring well for the increasing productivity of the Filipino workforce. They are, however, a minuscule portion of the labour force. The Philippine banking system is underdeveloped, and credit availability is comparable to the level in Indonesia, a regional peer with similarly weak banking. There is need for more rapid growth in these activities, although the majority of jobs in brick-and-mortar retail banking are low value added.

If we look at the evolution of the entire labour force using the statistics of the International Labor Organisation, there are grounds for optimism.

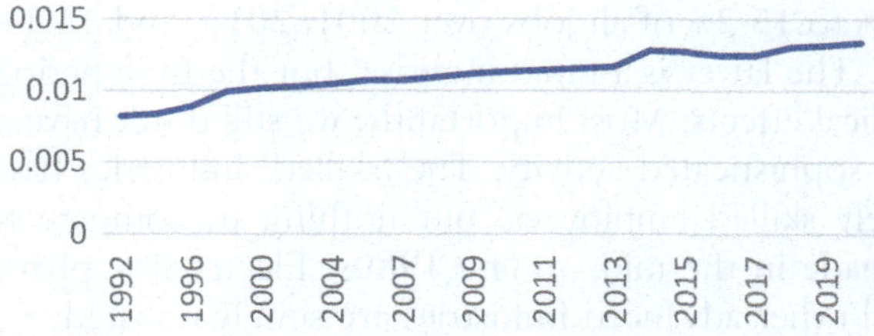

Fig. 3.18 Philippine employment in finance and insurance activities (*Data source* ILOSTAT labour force statistics)

Imposing a rather inaccurate division into skilled (managers, professionals, technicians and associate professionals) and unskilled (service and sales workers, craft and related trades workers, plant and machine operators, and assemblers, and alimentary occupations and skilled agricultural, forestry and fishery workers) upon ILO occupation categories, there is a growth from 19 to 40% for skilled occupations of the entire labour force.

This appears to contradict the growing GDP contribution of low productivity work. Part of the problem is that none of the classifications schemes—large occupational groups of the ILO (International Labour Organisation), PSA (2019) (Philippine Statistical Authority) industries of the economy contributing to GDP or activities contributing to unemployment—clearly discriminate between high skill or low skill employment. The mostly unskilled *occupations* remain at 60% of the workforce. Again, even in 2019, persons classified as self-employed without employees or working without pay are 32.9% of the work force.

Another way to evaluate the trend to higher skilled work is to group industries as higher or lower skilled. The data available makes this somewhat difficult as there are no categories for electronics or computers (although Cherry is a Philippine manufacturer of tablets and smartphones), for pharmaceuticals and biological products (there are 47 members of the Pharmaceutical Association of the Philippines, although perhaps most of the sophisticated work takes place outside of the country), nor for software publishing or programming (the Philippine software association has over 100 corporate members, albeit many with foreign brand names and active in industries using software such as telecommunications, cloud services and consulting). Grouping as skilled the available categories of chemicals, machinery (non-electrical and electrical) and transport equipment, we get a growth in skilled employment from 14.00% to 15.2% of all jobs over 2001–2013, and 14.1–15.2% over 2010–2013. The latter is a rapid increase, but the time period is perhaps open to cyclical effects. Most importantly, we still don't have an indicator of the most sophisticated activity. The 'skilled' industries have a portion of moderately skilled employees, but nothing to compare to the push Singapore made in the mid- to late 1980s. Electronics, pharmaceuticals, software and other advanced industries are simply unlisted.

World Bank (2018) includes such positive affirmations as 'a resurgence in manufacturing raises labor productivity' (page 45) and 'rapid labor productivity growth in the service sector despite its dual nature' (page 48). These assertions are true. For example, manufacture productivity, about 50% higher than services, is increasing and has very slightly increased its share of GDP since 2009. Figure 4.2 of the report suggests that the manufacturing sector is transitioning to more skill-intensive production… if one is willing to accept that furniture and food manufacture are more skill intensive than the manufacture of textiles, wearing apparel, and petroleum and other fuel products. This last category of petroleum and other fuels products is capital intensive. Manufacturing labour tends to be more productive as it becomes capital intensive. In services this is not necessarily the case. Most services become more productive as skills increase—such as in finance and software. Once technology is good enough, skill is the determinating factor. Although Figure 4.2 has a quantitative basis, it really depends upon several qualitative judgements about industries are more skill intensive (for example, chemicals versus petroleum; some speciality chemicals could conceivably require more skill than fuel production). However, if 'skill' is being used as a synonym of labour intensive, then 'Figure 4.2' would suggest that manufacture in the Philippines is becoming less capital intensive—not necessarily a good sign.

Rodrik has observed that a premature de-industrialisation is occurring in developing countries worldwide. He surmised that globalisation was part of the explanation. A comparison of the contribution of manufacturing to GDP in the Philippines and Vietnam at first seems to be an instance supporting his conjecture, as the relatively closed economy of the Philippines derives a higher portion of GDP from manufacture than does the open economy of Vietnam (see Fig. 3.19).

A more detailed examination of both policy and GDP statistics, however, undermines this support. When we add mining, construction, electricity, water and gas utilities to complete the gamut of industry

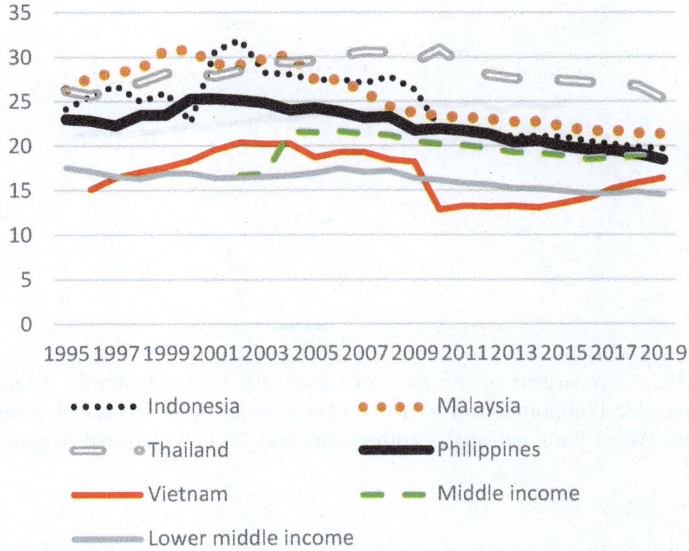

Fig. 3.19 Manufacture as a percentage of GDP compared (*Data sources* World Bank national accounts data, and OECD National Accounts data files)

beyond manufacture, then Vietnam exhibits a slightly higher portion of GDP from industry than does the Philippines (see Fig. 3.20 *Industry as % GDP Philippines and Vietnam compared*). Again, a much higher portion of Vietnam's GDP is generated by agriculture fisheries and forestry. If we exclude this sector and compare the ratios of industry to services for both countries, the Philippines appear clearly more 'de-industrialised' than Vietnam as Fig. 3.20 reveals. Further, the manufacturing value-added ratio for Vietnam has been on a rapid increase since 2010, while the same ratio in the Philippines has been in decline since 2000. The drop in importance of Vietnam manufacture ten years ago can be ascribed to the global financial crisis that reduced both demand and investment. The relatively open and globalised economy of Vietnam has not de-industrialised, and arguably is becoming more industrial, while the relatively isolated economy of the Philippines, 'protected' from globalisation, has prematurely become a service economy.

Perhaps this evidence could be rejected. Since this trend is becoming more marked, it could be argued that opening the Philippine economy to

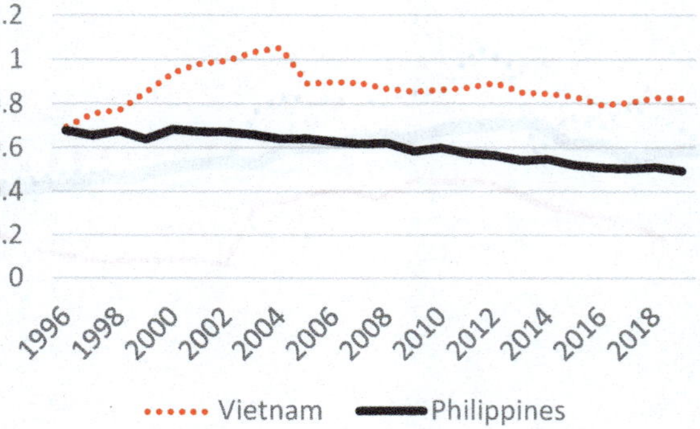

Fig. 3.20 Comparison of the ratio of value-added by industry to value-added by services for Philippines and Vietnam (*Data source* Author's calculations using data from World Bank national accounts data and OECD National Accounts data files)

globalizing influences was the cause, as Rodrik suggested for developing nations in general. An examination of the expenditure components of GDP reveals a different story for the Philippines.

Analysis Using the Expenditure Approach to GDP

Figure 3.21 shows the evolution of the different expenditure components of Philippine GDP since 1995.

The visual impression is that investment (gross capital formation as a percent of GDP) is a mirror image of the mostly negative net exports (external balance on goods and services as a percent of GDP). This seems to suggest that, in order to invest more, the country should either export less and or import more. This contradicts common sense, and an increasingly negative trade balance does not seem to be very good policy advice. Closer examination reveals a different insight.

The total of household and government consumption is almost constant and represents almost 85% of GDP. This leaves less than 15% for investment when trade is balanced, far less than even stable advanced economies are investing, and several times less than the historic rates of the Asian tigers and dragons of Singapore, Hong Kong, South Korea, Taiwan, Japan and China in their periods of rapid growth. However, it

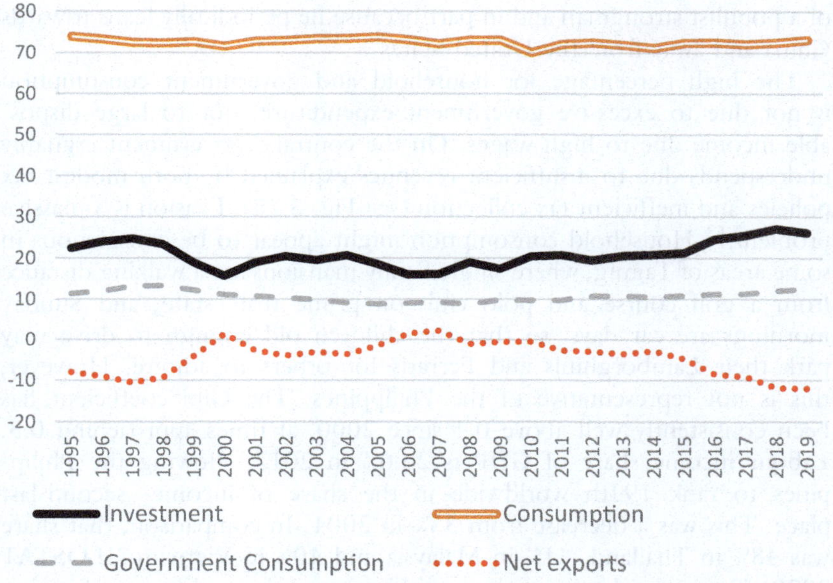

Fig. 3.21 Expenditure side components of GDP (*Data source* World Bank national accounts data, and OECD National Accounts data files)

is to be expected since the Philippines have been short of capital since World War II.

This was also the case of Vietnam at the start of the 1990s. As in the Philippines, government revenues from taxes are low (although more by policy than by evasion and ineffective collection). Like the Philippines, Vietnam had a negative trade balance for many years. However, capital formation (investment) in Vietnam was one third to one half higher than in the Philippines as a portion of GDP, up until the Duterte administration in the Philippines. The difference is foreign direct investment. Successive government administrations in the Philippines did not allow outside financing into the country until very timid changes beginning in the 1990s. FDI inflows increased from 0.4% of GDP in 1992 and reached a peak of 2.5% in 1994. It then dropped down until jumping to 3.2% after the Asian financial crisis. It has breached 3% only once since then. The increase in investment since the arrival of Duterte is strictly domestic, perhaps in part because foreign media present his administration as that of a populist strongman and in part because he periodically leans towards China and away from the United States.

The high percentage for household and government consumption is not due to excessive government expenditure, nor to large disposable income due to high wages. On the contrary, government arguably underspends due to insufficient revenues explained by both modest tax policies and inefficient tax collection (see Fig. 3.22). Evasion is a massive problem.[12] Household consumption might appear to be conspicuous in some areas of Taguig, where single family mansions are a walking distance from a golf course and polo club on prime real estate, and Sunday mornings are car days, so that the children old enough to drive may park their Lamborghinis and Ferraris for others to admire. However, this is not representative of the Philippines. The Gini coefficient has been consistently well above 0.4 since 2000, at times approaching 0.5. Labour income share of GDP is 26.6% in 2017, allowing the Philippines to rank 194th worldwide in the share of income—second-last place. This was a decrease from 33% in 2004. In comparison, that share was 48% in Thailand, 41% in Malaysia and 40% in Vietnam (ILOSTAT 2020). Switzerland, one of the wealthiest countries and best performing

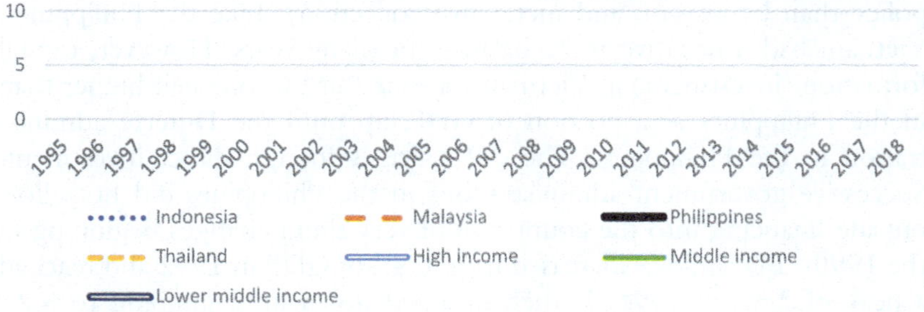

Fig. 3.22 Government revenue as a percentage of GDP compared (*Data sources* International Monetary Fund, Government Finance Statistics Yearbook and data files, and World Bank and OECD GDP estimates)

economies worldwide, posted a share of 70.6% for 2017. Since government revenue share of GDP was about 15% in 2017 and 2018, how can household plus government reach 85% of GDP? A healthy portion of household consumption is financed by non-(domestic) labour income: the revenue of the very rich, and remittances from overseas Filipino workers. These are Filipinos who leave their children and spouses behind to seek work in other countries, because the domestic Filipino economy does not provide them jobs with sufficient income to live decent lives. If we exclude countries with a population under 10 million, the Philippines had the highest remittances as percentage of GDP in the world until surpassed by the Ukraine in 2016. Ukraine remittances have been increasing dramatically since the start of military conflicts there in 2014 (see Fig. 3.23). In 2019, personal remittances to the Philippines were US$35 billion, or 9.33% of GDP.

About two percent of Filipinos manage to work abroad, sometimes in deplorable conditions and after covering their overseas expenses, and remit amounts equivalent up to 10% of the expenditure capacity of the

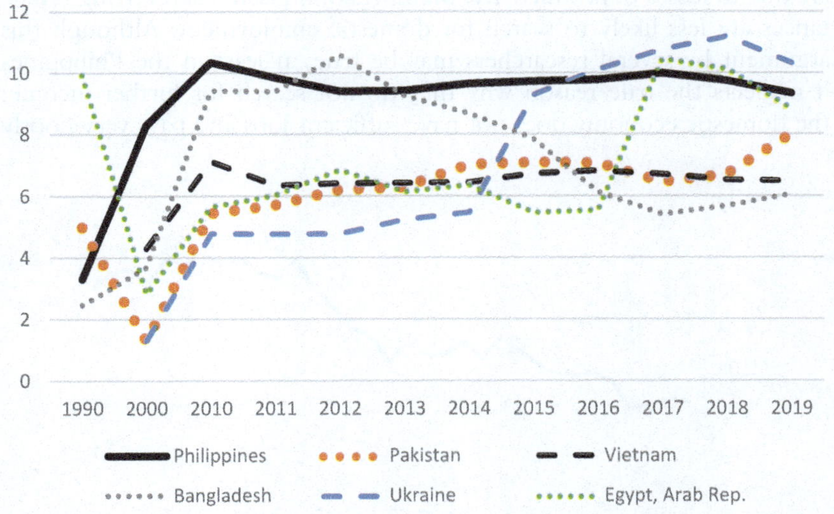

Fig. 3.23 Personal remittances in larger countries received as a percentage of GDP (*Data sources* World Bank staff estimates based on IMF balance of payments data, and World Bank and OECD GDP estimates)

domestic economy. Notably, this factor increased from 3.3% to 10% of the economy over 1990–2010, and from current US$ 5 billion in 1998 to $35 billion in 2019. These $35 billion are equivalent to 9.33% of GDP, increasing the purchasing power of the large segment of a population otherwise limited to the 26.6% share of GDP for labour income. Since remittances were 9.33% of GDP, while domestic wages were the equivalent of 26.6% of GDP, so that remittances were 37% as important of total wages paid to all employees in the Philippines. Figure 3.24 shows that the number of persons working abroad varied from 2% of total employment to a peak of 6% in 2008, with 5% in 2019 remitting that amount equal to 37% of wages—overseas work had ten times the earning power of domestic work *after* covering all expenses.

The growth in remittances brought an increase of purchasing power equivalent to 15% of the GDP growth from 1998 to 2019. Analytical and empirical work on the impact remittances on growth in other countries has returned mixed results, from far greater than 'addition' to demand, to slowing growth (Bayangos and Jansen 2009; Chami et al. 2003; Dridi et al. 2019; Meyer and Shera 2017; Sutradhar 2020). The negative effects are due to losses of productivity. Members of households receiving remittances are less likely to search for domestic employment. Although this argument by several researchers may be true, at least in the Philippines it neglects the true reason why they do not search for further income: the domestic economy does not have sufficient jobs and pays very poorly

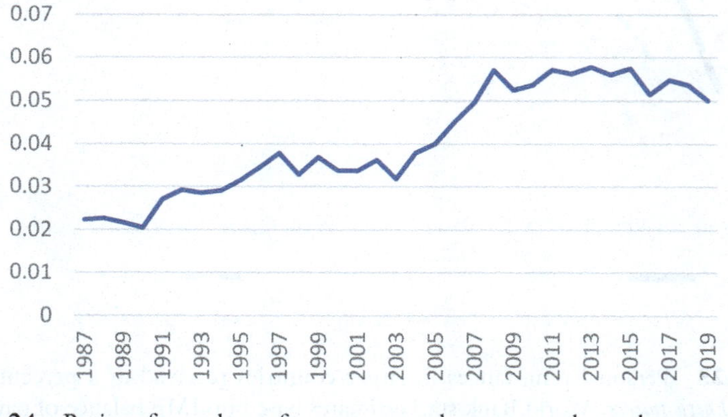

Fig. 3.24 Ratio of number of overseas workers to total employment (*Data source* International Labour Organisation, ILOSTAT database)

(see Battistella 1995). A vibrant economy would provide incentive to work even for members of households receiving remittances. Further, on the ground and away from the computer terminal, these 'household members' are often either the children or the parents of overseas workers. Whatever the case, the undeniable multiplier effect of remittance cash injection remains. A conservative 1.6 multiplier suggests that a quarter of economic growth on the demand side is explained by remittances. This corresponds well with the importance of the retail contribution on the supply side.

Conclusion

The Philippine economy remained relatively stagnant from independence on July 4, 1946 until the mid-1990s in spite of some shake up during the Marcos administration.

GDP per capita barely moved compared to the growth of neighbouring nations. The composition of GDP production did change over time, but the contribution of industry eventually ended at the same level as it began. Industry contribution to GDP in grew from 30.2% in 1949 to 35.6% in 1995, but would drop to 30% by 2015. It did surpass 40% for a decade under Marcos, financed by debt. The Philippines did not experience the kind of industrialisation found in the transition of the Asian Tigers to richer economies. Services, rather than industry replaced and even mirrored the decreasing portion of GDP contributed by agriculture, forestry and fisheries. Although population moved from the countryside to urban areas from 1960 to 1990, industry could not absorb this number of new employees, and most ended up in low-paying service jobs from 1980 (the peak year for industry under Marcos) onward.

At first glance, the economy has boomed since the 1990s, ranking among the top five to ten fast growing economies of large countries since the global financial crisis—measured on a GDP-per capita basis. Closer examination uncovers some unpleasant facts.

Rural population remained at about 53% from 1990 to 2019. The work of people in the country side was and is terribly mismanaged, thanks to repeatedly unenforced land reforms, distorted marketing channels from farmer to city consumer, and poor policy (see for example Mendoza [2021]). Recent investment data is not available, but at the turn of the century the Philippines had less than half (117) as many tractors per hundred square kilometers of arable land as did Vietnam (262). Philippine sugar and rice exports have been replaced by sugar, rice and other agricultural imports.

Services grew from 50 to 60% of the economy. Although there is some good news thanks to the business process outsourcing sector not being restricted from foreign investment nor from exporting to lucrative markets, growth in services and lessening relative importance of agriculture and fishing could lead to the relative impoverishment of a large portion of the population rather than the blossoming of new, high value-added jobs. Retail 'Trade and Repair of Motor Vehicles, Motorcycles, Personal and Household Goods' have accounted for 30% of services from 2006 to 2017, while financial intermediation, a mix of both high value and low paying jobs, grew from 11 to 13% of services but still only 7.3% of the economy.[13]

An outsized portion of GDP growth on the production side was in the retail trade and business process outsourcing—both businesses with little or no restriction on foreign investment, and the latter of which is one-third export oriented.

This suggests that the Philippines economy was stagnant from 1960 to 1995 because of isolation from foreign trade and investment, and grew—rapidly but with weaknesses—from 1995 to 2019 because of modest opening to foreign investment and trade. The effect of the isolation from 1960 to 1995 was all the stronger because the Philippines, severely damaged during the Second World War, saw much of the war compensation and aid rendered less effective by the impact of the free trade with the United States of America at an unfair exchange rate. Thereafter, the Philippines abstained from exports and foreign direct investment could have brought in much needed capital. Although the economy has been timidly opening since the 1990s, there remains little incentive to invest in capital intensive manufacture (Magnoli 2008).

Lack of capital alone was not and is not the only problem. Government and business are conducted in a feudal-like culture where the immediate quid-pro-quo interest of each actor is maximised rather than the good of the country. This is only viable in the absence of competition and benefits mainly the rich and powerful—and perhaps even these less than they would benefit from a more robust economy.

Perhaps this paints too stark and negative a picture of an economy that remains one of the fastest growing of among those of the world's large populations. Filipinos show initiative in opportunity and in adversity. Certainly, the poor and the (now larger and growing) middle class are better off today than 20 years ago. The 2018 Family Income and Expenditure Survey is filled with good news that on the average Filipino household is able to save part of its income across all deciles by income per capita. As Table 3.5 indicates, the income increase from 2015 to 2018 was 20% for the lowest decile, 15% for the next, 14% for the next and so on down to 4% for the second-highest income and little more than 0% for highest income, resulting in a reduction in the Gini coefficient down to 0.42. The poorest decile began to save, while savings tripled for the next decile.

However, many Filipinos work long hours and then spend long hours in ridiculous traffic, most often packed cheek-to-jowl in jeepneys before returning home after transferring several times in a fragmented transportation network. Some families are financed by members working abroad for most of the year. Sadly, in many other families some members use gambling and shabu to flee desperate situations. The 2020 (and 2021) pandemic has been devastating for the economy of the Philippines. Not only have lockdowns and curfews prevented many from working domestically, but remittance income has shrunk dramatically.

The Philippines are the only Christian and Catholic society in the region, and perhaps the most truly Catholic population in the world (were World Bank to compile a statistic such as the portion of church goers without a seat because they did not arrive 15 minutes early). However, it is hard to imagine an economy farther removed from the ideal of the social doctrine of the Catholic Church. Filipinos deserve better.

Table 3.5 Summary of the 2018 Family Income and Expenditure Survey

	2018				*2012*				*Change 2012 to 2018*		
Per Capita Income Decile	*Income*	*Expenditure*	*Savings*	*Savings as % income (%)*	*Income*	*Expenditure*	*Savings*	*Savings as % income (%)*	*Income (%)*	*Expenditure (%)*	*Savings as % income (%)*
1	97	93	4	4	81	83	− 3	− 4	20	12	− 233
2	123	111	12	10	107	103	4	4	15	8	200
3	143	125	18	13	125	114	10	8	14	10	80
4	168	144	24	14	147	132	16	11	14	9	50
5	192	161	31	16	171	151	20	12	12	7	55
6	224	184	40	18	205	178	27	13	9	3	48
7	263	211	53	20	243	204	40	16	8	3	33
8	316	242	74	23	299	244	55	18	6	− 1	35
9	406	300	106	26	390	307	84	22	4	− 2	26
10	740	465	275	37	737	501	236	32	0	− 7	17
Total	2672	2036	637	24	2505	2017	489	20	7	1	30

Note All non-percentage units are in thousand 2012 pesos
Source PSA [2020d]

Notes

1. The decree ended the *situado*: 'In addition to trade goods and silver remitted in exchange for Asian goods, the galleons also carried a *situado* from the treasury of the viceroyalty of New Spain to the colony of the Philippines. This *situado* supplemented tributes and duties collected by the colonial administration of the Philippines out of which they paid the salaries of officials, military expenses, the building of fortifications, and other public expenses. (…) without a subsidy from the mineral wealth of New Spain, Spain would not have been able to finance the defense and colonisation of the Philippines (…)' (Bjork 1998, which provides a more detailed and rigorous description).
2. The main irritants were free trade at the pre-war exchange rate and American citizens having the same rights as Filipinos in the exploitation of natural resources (agricultural, energy, mineral) etc. as stipulated in articles V and VII of Commonwealth Act number 733.
3. This is different from the Barry Eichengreen, Ricardo Hausmann and Ugo Panizza notion of original sin in economics. Sicat (2018) calls the restrictive provisions of the Philippine constitution the original sin of the Philippine economy.
4. Detailed data on tariffs can be obtained using two tools available at https://www.wto.org/english/tratop_e/tariffs_e/tariff_data_e.htm.
5. Indonesia is the only member nation of ASEAN with data on the World Bank Services Trade Restrictiveness Index.
6. Admittedly, this is true for ASEAN in general. See ASEAN-EU (2019).
7. Here are excerpts from article XIII:

   Section 10. The Congress shall, upon recommendation of the economic and planning agency, when the national interest dictates, reserve to citizens of the Philippines or to corporations or associations at least sixty per centum of whose capital is owned by such citizens, or such higher percentage as Congress may prescribe, certain areas of investments. The Congress shall enact measures that will encourage the formation and operation of enterprises whose capital is wholly owned by Filipinos. In the grant of rights, privileges and concessions covering the national economy and patrimony, the State shall give preference to qualified Filipinos.

The State shall regulate and exercise authority over foreign investments within its national jurisdiction and in accordance with its national goals and priorities.

Section 11. No franchise, certificate or any other form of authorisation for the operation of a public utility shall be granted except to citizens of the Philippines or to corporations or associations organised under the laws of the Philippines, at least sixty per centum of whose capital is owned by such citizens; nor shall such franchise, certificate or authorisation be exclusive in character or for a longer period than fifty years. Neither shall any such franchise or right be granted except under the condition that it shall be subject to amendment, alteration or repeal by the Congress when the common good so requires. The State shall encourage equity participation in public utilities by the general public. The participation of foreign investors in the governing body of any public utility enterprise shall be limited to their proportionate share in its capital, and all the executive and managing officers of such corporation or association must be citizens of the Philippines.

Section 12. The State shall promote the preferential use of Filipino labor, domestic materials and locally produced goods, and adopt measures that help make them competitive.

Section 14: The practice of all professions in the Philippines shall be limited to Filipino citizens, save in cases prescribed by law.

8. Philippines is formally a democracy but nearly feudal in practice. This is still true today, but was more deeply so in the twentieth century. Votes were acquired by money, short-term favours, false promises, 'friendly explanations and advice' offered to bewildered voters, and voter fraud perpetrated by political hangers on. A large portion of electors had little sense of the 'good of the nation' or a political opinion, but rather made their vote according to a personal (or familial) quid pro quo (see Hutchcraft 2000, 2003, 2017 for one Westerner's appreciation of politics in the Philippines). The end result was political dominance by a number of rich families. The change in the families benefiting from the economy would eventually lead to the downfall of Marcos. Much is made of the People Power revolution in the Philippines. Unlike the French and American revolutions, it was bloodless. Like them, it

mobilised virtually the entire population and is seen as a triumph as good over evil. Like the French revolution, however, it was also a revolution that put one class of society in control in the place of another group (the aristocracy in France and Marco's cronies in the Philippines). It did not lead to a new spring time for the Filipino people. It did lead to a new spring time for a number of Filipino family dynasties who remain influential today (Mendoza 2016a, 2019) is the principle researcher on the topic of the dominant family 'dynasties'; for more on family dynasties and 'oligarchs' in the Philippines, see also Alba 2007; Anderson 1988; Calonzo 2020; Cardenas 2019; Chanco 2020; Chikiamco 2020; Clarete et al. 2018; Conde 2007; Fabella 2020; Jiao 2019). The current Duterte phenomenon is in part a struggle between these families and him, a relative newcomer. The presentation in foreign media of the Philippines in general and the Duterte administration in particular owes much to the oligarchs influence upon the media. Thus, the West knows that under Duterte, ABS-CBN did not have its license renewed in 2020. Most in the West do not know that ABS-CBN did not follow due process, had not paid taxes and, providing personal motive just before the 2016 election, accepted payment from Duterte for a political advertisement, but then showed instead a critical announcement, putting a negative script into the mouths of children (see Lema 2016; Yap 2020). Although the media of many countries has made much of the political spectacle that has been unfolding in the United States of America, this kind of squabbling and mis-information has been part and parcel of the Philippines for decades.

9. Quite possibly, a few corporations lobbied strongly enough to influence the decision in a way that would have been repugnant to many Americans had they been aware of it. For political manoeuvring to pass the act in the Philippines, see Shalom (1980).
10. The ecological issues are not discussed here. The problem with nuclear power is *risk* of extreme environmental problems. The Three Mile Island incident (1979) and the Chernobyl disaster (1986) contributed to the Aquino administration's resistance. In reality, the risk seems to have well-managed by the project's engineering, as subsequent volcanic eruptions and earthquakes have not damaged the structures that were built. The passage of time has been more brutal.

11. Low productivity because the work is not highly valued *economically*. Social work and teaching are perhaps of great value to society, but we do not value them when we reach for our cheque books. It is also true that much of the time of sales clerks is spent waiting for customers, although an able store manager will have his or her employees sort, repackage, take inventory and so on during off periods. However, slow economies mean store clerks have more time on their hands. A personal 2010 visit to a mall retail store in Cambodia brought this home: seven or eight sales clerks for one lone customer. The drive back to my hotel passed an area with multiple print shops. Outside each were employees seated at wooden tables with samples of letterhead and business cards on show. Again, no customers. The mall experience in the Philippines, Indonesia and even Vietnam is dramatically different. Filipinos love to walk in malls as this provides an opportunity to socialise, usually with free air conditioning. However, although all love to shop as well, most have limited purchasing power. Thus, the busiest establishments in the Mall of Asia are McDonalds, Starbucks (to look upscale) and Jolibee.
12. Western journalists and several freedom indices blacklisted the Duterte regime for persecuting ABS-CBN, presenting its behavior as 'skillful tax avoidance'.
13. The 2006–2017 statistics are from PSA (2021). The Philippine Statistical Authority is inconsistent in its presentation of data, perhaps as different political administrations wished to highlight different aspects of the economy. For example, the classification of services into sectors differs for 1990–2014 and 2008–2018. Health services are omitted from both classifications. Information technology-related services are not explicitly named, but perhaps are part of 'Real Estate, Renting & Business Activity' in the latest classification.

References

Alba, Michael M. 2007. Why Has the Philippines Remained a Poor Country? Some Perspectives from Growth Economics. *Philippine Review of Economics* 4 (2).

Anderson, Benedict. 1988. Cacique Democracy in the Philippines: Origins and Dreams. *New Left Review* I (169) (May–June): 3–31.

ASEAN-EU. 2019. Non-Tariff Barriers (NTBs) in ASEAN and Their Elimination from a Business Perspective. A Link to the Document is available at http://asiantradecentre.org/talkingtrade/tackling-non-tariff-barriers-in-asean. Accessed September 9, 2020.

Bayangos, Veronica, and Karel Jansen. 2009 The Macroeconomics of Remittances in the Philippines. Institute of Social Studies. Working Paper 470

Battistella, G. 1995. Philippine Overseas Labour: From Export to Management. *ASEAN Economic Bulletin* 12 (2): 257–273.

Bjork, Katharine. 1998. The Link That Kept the Philippines Spanish: Mexican Merchant Interests and the Manila Trade, 1571–1815. *Journal of World History* 9 (1): 25–50.

Bolt, Jutta, Robert Inklaar, Herman de Jong, and Jan Luiten van Zanden. 2018. Rebasing 'Maddison': New Income Comparisons and the Shape of Long-Run Economic Development. Maddison Project Working Paper, nr. 10. Available for download at www.ggdc.net/maddison. Accessed November 28, 2020.

Calonzo, Andreo, Claire Jiao, and Ditas Lopez. 2020. Duterte Takes on Philippine Elite and Ends Up Even more Popular. Bloomberg, January 27.

Cardenas, Kenneth. 2019. The Mobility-Oligopoly Nexus in Philippine Property Development. In *Mobilities of Labour and Capital in Asia: Spatialities, Institutions, and Cultures*, ed. P.S. Aulakh and P.F. Kelly. Cambridge: Cambridge University Press.

Chami, R., C. Fullenkamp, and S. Jahjah. 2003. Are Immigrant Remittances Flow a Source of Capital for Development? IMF Working Paper 03/189.

Chanco, Boo. 2020. Tools of the Oligarchs. Foundation for Economic Freedom. Available at https://www.fef.org.ph/boo-chanco/tools-of-theoligarchs/. Accessed November 5, 2021.

Chikiamco, Calixto. 2020. The Oligarchy During the Marcos Regime and its Economic Impact. Foundation for Economic Freedom. Available at https://www.fef.org.ph/calixto-chikiamco/the-oligarchy-during-the-marcos-regime-and-its-economic-impact/. Accessed December 29, 2020.

Clarete, Ramon L., Emmanuel F. Esguerra, and Hal Hill. 2018. The Filipino Economy: An Overview. In *The Philippine Economy: No Longer the East Asian Exception?*, eds. Ramon L. Clarete, Emmanuel F. Esguerra and Hal Hill. Singapore: ISEAS—Yusof Ishak Institute.

Conde, Carlos. 2007. Family Dynasties Bind Politics in Philippines. *The New York Times*, May 11.

Dolan, Ronald E., ed. 1991. *Philippines: A Country Study*. Washington, DC: GPO for the Library of Congress.

Dridi, Jemma, Tunc Gursoy, Hector Perez-Saiz, and Mounir Bari. 2019. The Impact of Remittances on Economic Activity: The Importance of Sectoral Linkages. IMF Working Paper WP/19/175. International Monetary Fund.

Erbe, Rainer. 1982. Foreign Indebtedness and Economic Growth: The Philippines. *Intereconomics, Verlag Weltarchiv, Hamburg* 17 (3): 125–132.

Eurostat. 2020. Distributive trade statistics - NACE Rev. 2. https://ec.europa.eu/eurostat/statistics-explained/index.php/Distributive_trade_statistics_-_NACE_Rev._2#Structural_profile. Accessed September 13, 2020.

Fabella, Raul V. 2020. Who Is an Oligarch? A Taxonomy from One Ruminant's Backside. *Business World*, August 16. Available at https://www.bworldonline.com/who-is-anoligarch-a-taxonomy-from-one-ruminants-backside/. Accessed November 5, 2021.

Feenstra, Robert C., Robert Inklaar, and Marcel P. Timmer. 2015. The Next Generation of the Penn World Table. *American Economic Review* 105 (10): 3150–3182. Available for download at www.ggdc.net/pwt. Accessed December 12, 2020.

Hutchcroft, P. 2000. Obstructive Corruption: The Politics of Privilege in the Philippines. In *Rents, Rent-Seeking and Economic Development: Theory and Evidence in Asia*, ed. M. Khan and K. Jomo, 207–247. Cambridge: Cambridge University Press. https://doi.org/10.1017/CBO9781139085052.006.

Hutchcraft, Paul D., and Joel Rocamora. 2003. Strong Demands and Weak Institutions: The Origins and Evolution of the Democratic Deficit in the Philippines. *Journal of East Asian Studies* 3: 259–292.

Hutchcraft, Paul D. 2017. Linking Capital and Countryside: Patronage and Clientelism in Japan, Thailand, and the Philippines. *Public Policy* XVI and XVII: 52–77.

ILOSTAT. 2020. Labour Income Share as a Percent of GDP. Table available at https://www.ilo.org/shinyapps/bulkexplorer27/?lang=en&segment=indicator&id=EMP_2EMP_SEX_OCU_NB_A. Accessed September 15, 2020.

ILOSTAT. 2021. Employment by Sex and Economic Activity -- ILO Modelled Estimates. International Labour Organization. Available at https://ilostat.ilo.org/data/. Accessed January 20, 2021.

Jiao, Claire, Andreo Calonzo, and Hannah Dormido. 2019. A Power Shift Is Under Way in Duterte's Game of Thrones. Bloomberg, June 8.

Lema, Karen. 2016. Philippine Court Halts Rare TV Attack ad Showing Kids Against Duterte. *Reuters*, May 6. Available at https://www.reuters.com/article/us-philippines-election-court-idUSKCN0XX0SO. Accessed January 26, 2021.

Lindsey, Charles W. 1987. The Philippine state and transnational investment. *Bulletin of Concerned Asian Scholars* 19 (2): 24–41. https://doi.org/10.1080/14672715.1987.104098.

LPI. 2020. The Logistics Performance Index 2018. World Bank. Download links available at https://lpi.worldbank.org. Accessed September 16, 2020.

Magnoli Bocchi, Alessandro. 2008. Rising Growth, Declining Investment: The Puzzle of the Philippines. Policy Research Working Paper 4472. The World Bank

McCoy, Alfred W. 2009. The Philippine Oligarchy at the Turn of the Twenty-First Century. In *An Anarchy of Families: State and Family in the Philippines*, ed. A.W. McCoy. Madison: University of Wisconsin Press.

Mendoza, Ronald U., Edsel L. Beja Jr, Victor S. Venida, and David B. Yap. 2016a. Political Dynasties and Poverty: Measurement and Evidence of Linkages in the Philippines. *Oxford Development Studies* 44 (2): 189–201.

Mendoza, Ronald U., Yla Gloria Marie P. Paras, and Donald Jay Bertulfo. 2016b. The Bataan Nuclear Power Plant in the Philippines: Lessons from a White Elephant Project. Ateneo School of Government, Working Document 16-001. Available at https://papers.ssrn.com/sol3/papers.cfm?abstract_id=2833766. Accessed January 6, 2021.

Mendoza, Ronald U., Leonardo M. Jaminola III, and Jurel K. Yap. 2019. From Fat to Obese: Political Dynasties after the 2019 Midterm Elections. Available at SSRN https://papers.ssrn.com/sol3/papers.cfm?abstract_id=3449201 or https://doi.org/10.2139/ssrn.3449201. Accessed November 5, 2021.

Mendoza, Teodoro C. 2021. PH Descent from Sugar Exporter to Importer: What Happened? Inquirer.net Available at https://business.inquirer.net/315286/ph-descent-from-sugar-exporter-to-importer-what-happened#ixzz6ivYAUxax. Accessed January 8, 2021.

Meyer, Dietmar, and Adela Shera. 2017. The Impact of Remittances on Economic Growth: An Econometric Model. *Economia* 18: 147–155.

Moses, Bernard. 1893. The Economic Condition of Spain in the Sixteenth Century. *Journal of Political Economy* 1: 513–534.

PSA. 2019. Preliminary Results of the 2019 Annual Estimates of Labor Force Survey. Philippine Statistics Authority. Available at http://www.psa.gov.ph/content/preliminary-results-2019-annual-estimates-labor-force-survey-lfs. Accessed September 15, 2020.

PSA. 2020a. Table 1.1 Gross Domestic Product, by Major Industry. As of April 2020. Philippine Statistics Authority.

PSA. 2020b. Table 2.3 Gross Domestic Product, by Major Industry. Percent Share to GDP, at Constant 2018 Prices. As of April 2020. Philippine Statistics Authority.

PSA. 2020c. 2017. Annual Survey of Philippine Business and Industry (ASPBI) - Information Technology -Business Process Management (IT-BPM) Sector: Final Results. Available at https://psa.gov.ph/content/2017-annual-survey-philippine-business-and-industry-aspbi-information-technology-business. Accessed September 12, 2020

PSA. 2020d. 2018 Family Income and Expenditure Survey. Philippine Statistic Authority. Available at https://psa.gov.ph/content/family-income-and-expenditure-survey-fies-0. Accessed January 19, 2021.

PSA 2021. Gross Domestic Product at Constant 2000 Prices. Available at https://openstat.psa.gov.ph/PXWeb/pxweb/en/DB/DB__3E__CH__MA/

0073E3D2B10.px/table/tableViewLayout1/?rxid=35760b55-d597-46ac-a3a5-1051a3cfbd4c. Accessed March 9, 2021.

PSA. n.d. Survey on Overseas Filipinos (SOF). Available at https://psa.gov.ph/content/survey-overseas-filipinos-sof? Accessed January 6, 2021.

PSA OpenStat. 2020. Gross National Income and Gross Domestic Product, by Industry Tables constructable at http://openstat.psa.gov.ph/PXWeb/pxweb/en/DB/DB__2B__NA__AN__1SUM/0052B5CPRA1.px/?rxid=968e7cd8-2cfc-4de8-af1d-63f32e87c69f. Accessed September 15, 2020.

Reyes, Cecilia. 2019. Philippine Non-Tariff Measures Project. Chapter 7 in Non-Tariff Measures -An Update. Economic research Institute for ASEAN and Asia(ERI).

Stats NZ. 2019. Which Industries Contributed to New Zealand's GDP? https://www.stats.govt.nz/experimental/which-industries-contributed-to-new-zealands-gdp. Accessed September 13, 2020.

Shalom, Stephen R. 1980. Philippine Acceptance of the Bell Trade Act of 1946: A Study of Manipulatory Democracy. Pacific Historical Review, 499–517.

Sicat, Gerardo P. 2008. Philippine Economic Nationalism. *The Philippine Review of Economics* 45 (2).

Sicat, Gerardo P. 2018. American Private Direct Investment in the Philippines After Independence. *The Philippine Review of Economics* LII (2) (December 2015): 22–37.

Sicat, Gerardo P. 2019. Private Sector 1946–1950: Who Got War Damage Compensation? *Philippine Star*, April 19. Available at https://www.philstar.com/business/2019/04/17/1910568/private-sector-1946-1950-who-got-war-damage-compensation. Accessed November 5, 2021.

Sutradhar, Soma Rani. 2020. The Impact of Remittances on Economic Growth in Bangladesh, India, Pakistan and Sri Lanka. *International Journal of Economic Policy Studies* 14: 275–295.

WEF. 2017. GCI Dataset in Excel. World Economic Forum. http://reports.weforum.org/global-competitiveness-index-2017-2018/downloads/. Accessed January 21, 2021.

WEF. 2019. Global Competitiveness Report 2019. World Economic Forum.

WITS. 2020. Philippines Non-Tariff Measure (NTM) Summary. Available at https://wits.worldbank.org/tariff/non-tariff-measures/en/country/PHL. Accessed January 5, 2021.

World Bank. 2018. Growth and Productivity in the Philippines. Winning the Future. Available at http://documents1.worldbank.org/curated/en/586871537541775427/pdf/130056-REVISED-WB-Growth-and-Productivity-Full-Report-ONLINE.pdf. Accessed September 14, 2020.

Yap, D.J., Dona Z. Pazzibugan, Leila B. Salaverria, and Melvin Gascon. 2020. Duterte to ABS-CBN: Apology Accepted but Franchise Up to House. Inquirer, February 27. Available at https://newsinfo.inquirer.net/1233949/duterte-to-abs-cbn-apology-accepted-but-franchise-up-to-house. Accessed January 26, 2021.

CHAPTER 4

Open and Closed, Prosperity and Stagnation

Roderick Macdonald

Abstract Examination of the economy of Vietnam suggests that opening the economy can increase prosperity. Examination of the economy of the Philippines suggests that closing the economy leads to stagnation. The two countries in the world with the greatest hope of succeeding as an isolated economy are China and the United States. Due to resource costs and business incentives, China would face increased costs across its economy and slowed innovation even if given free access to world-wide intellectual property. The United States of America would also face increased costs and slowed innovation due to market size.

Keywords Open economy · Economic nationalism · Self-sufficiency · Growth · Remittances

An Overview of the Previous Chapters

International business in the twenty-first century is very different from that of the late eighteenth and early nineteenth centuries. We have moved beyond buying and selling goods across borders, and now trade, invest and produce goods and services across borders, as often as not crossing

R. Macdonald, *Open and Closed Economies*,
https://doi.org/10.1007/978-3-030-79534-4_4

two or more borders in any given chain of transactions. Still, the centuries old insights of Adam Smith and David Ricardo remain relevant.

Chapter 1 recalled the basic assertion of Smith and Ricardo that free trade is beneficial to the nation that welcomes it, as well as the common-sense notion that capital flowing into an economy will increase its capacity to produce wealth, and thus should also be beneficial. It put aside the question of mobility of labour as one that would be difficult to study, on the one hand, and, on the other hand, is not really entertained by world leaders preaching the 'open economy'.[1]

The introductory chapter then recognised that twentieth century economics research failed to confirm either (trade or capital) assertion. One reason for this is the complexity of economic reality, with far too many uncontrolled variables and too many waves of economic events to allow for either unbiased sampling or control for bias. Case studies, although not perfect, should permit some insight into the validity of the original assertions, and perhaps aid us to better formulate future research questions. The case study proposed contrasts the experience of the Philippines in the second half of the twentieth century with the experience of Vietnam in the first two decades of the twenty-first century. The former illustrates how a closing an economy leads to stagnation, while the latter illustrates how open an economy leads to growth.

Chapters 2 and 3 then examined the two economies.

Chapter 2 was able to demonstrate how opening up the economy of Vietnam led to rapid growth, but with two complications. The first complication was that the government only partially opened up the economy, as state-owned enterprises (SOEs) did not entertain foreign competition. This was not a major issue because the portion of the economy controlled by SOEs shrank, particularly in the first 20 years since Doi Moi, down to 25% of GDP in 2019. The second complication is that FDI has been into low value-producing activities, so that manufacturing labour is only marginally more productive than services labour even though services are almost entirely low value producing. This has led some empirical work, for example, Minh (2020), to results that suggest that FDI has had a negative impact upon the economic growth of Vietnam. However, it remains evident that manufacturing in Vietnam has expanded and the wealth of the nation increased dramatically. This is an instance that illustrates how empirical results require interpretation. Should we conclude that Vietnam would be wealthier without FDI, or that it has achieved such enviable growth in spite of foreign investment?

Rather than stop all future foreign investment, Vietnam needs to improve the terms of the FDI 'deal', perhaps to retain a higher portion of value created, but most importantly to incorporate foreign investment into an industrial strategy that upgrades labour productivity.

International trade is important for the economy of Vietnam and is responsible for much of its growth. FDI is also important, and linked both to exports and imports, which are the equivalent of 200% of GDP. This is very high for large territory economies, although far lower than the historically trade-based city-state economies of Singapore and Hong Kong. Surprisingly, the component of gross exports made up by domestic value added is only 56%, lower than Singapore's 61% and Hong Kong 75% (see Table 4.1). These higher percentages are explained in part by the importance of high-end business and financial services exported by both port cities. Vietnam faces the double challenge of building up supplier industries and cultivating higher value tradeable goods and services, with the goal of increasing the proportion of domestic value added.

The main argument of Chapter 3 was that the economy of the Philippines was stagnant in the second half of the twentieth century because it was closed to international trade and capital. That chapter also ran into complications. The first complication was the Marcos regime—an administration that accounted for a more than half of the 'comparator' years from 1960 to 1995. Marcos did open the economy somewhat to foreign capital, but tried to keep most ownership for himself and his cronies, so

Table 4.1 Domestic value added in gross exports as percent of GDP

	2005	*2006*	*2007*	*2008*	*2009*	*2010*	*2011*	*2012*	*2013*	*2014*	*2015*	*2016*
Japan	89.8	87.8	86.8	84.8	89.1	87.8	85.7	86.1	84.8	84.2	86.8	88.6
Korea	67.3	65.8	65.6	58.8	62.9	61.8	57.6	58.0	60.5	62.7	67.4	69.6
Hong Kong	72.4	70.5	69.4	67.3	70.9	68.4	67.6	68.1	69.0	70.8	73.4	75.2
India	81.2	79.4	79.3	75.5	78.2	76.4	74.9	74.9	75.3	77.1	80.9	83.9
Indonesia	81.6	85.1	85.7	85.0	87.9	87.6	87.2	86.7	86.1	85.9	87.1	88.7
Malaysia	55.0	56.6	55.9	59.7	60.2	59.4	60.6	61.9	62.8	63.4	63.1	63.9
Philippines	73.7	68.3	75.8	75.2	78.1	76.1	76.5	76.1	79.0	79.6	78.0	76.6
Singapore	57.2	55.4	58.6	54.8	58.0	58.7	56.5	56.2	57.2	57.0	59.1	60.6
Thailand	61.6	62.9	63.9	61.0	65.6	64.0	61.2	61.6	62.5	63.3	66.4	67.5
Viet Nam	63.9	61.9	59.2	58.5	62.8	59.5	58.2	59.2	58.3	57.6	55.5	56.4

Data source Trade in Value Added (TiVA): principal indicators

that much of the capital entered as loans to the government and crony business interests rather than as foreign direct investment. This led to growth for a few years, but ultimately the debt burden began to curb that growth, and the Marcos administration was unable to break with the overall post-war paralysis. The second complication is that subsequent years seem to belie the 'stagnation by isolation' lesson of the twentieth century. The Philippine economy has been growing since the mid-1990s, and especially in the last decade, in spite of very limited opening to trade and capital. This would seem to be a counter-example to the argument of this book. However, examination of the components of GDP on both the production and the expenditure sides showed that a significant part of that rapid growth is due to remittances spent on retail goods, resulting in an oversized retail industry (or perhaps an undersized remainder of the economy).

Minh (2020) found that remittances into Vietnam have a positive effect upon economic growth. At about 5–6% of GDP, these are considerable although just more than half the level in the Philippines. Further, given that Philippine domestic wages are a considerably smaller portion of GDP than in Vietnam, the impact of remittances upon demand is far greater in that country. Remittances into Vietnam and remittances into the Philippines differ in several ways, as indicated in Table 4.2. Personal remittances into Vietnam have a far more dramatic effect upon the individual receiving household, but at most half the impact upon the purchasing capacity of households in the overall economy.

Using a different approach, Nguyen (2017) had shown how remittances inflows into Vietnam have a detrimental effect by appreciating the national currency, making domestic production less competitive. His approach has not been applied recently to remittances into the Philippines, but a similar effect of appreciation is probable, although there is a smaller volume of exports to be affected.

Further Detail from the Philippines and Vietnam

The Philippines maintained a closed economy from before 1960 until the start of the Fidel Ramos presidency in 1992, with some partial exceptions during the Marcos regime. The result was a stagnant economy. Vietnam was completely closed off from the world by war and then a US-led embargo for most of the twentieth century until 1994. Policy changes

Table 4.2 Remittance profiles of Vietnam and The Philippines

	National income per capita	*Monthly income of recipient household*	*Number of workers abroad, in millions*	*Number of workers abroad as % population*	*Size of monthly remittances in 2019 US$*	*Remittance as % to recipient household domestic income*	*Remittances as % GDP*	*Labour wages as % GDP (2017)*	*Remittance % increase to household incomes*
Philippines	274	175	2.30	2.1	446	163	9.33	26.5	35.2
Vietnam	162	73	0.54	0.55%	735	453	6.49	40.5	16.0

Note All numbers are based on 2019 measurements, except labour wages as % GDP for which 2017 (the latest available) are used

Table 4.3 Principle sources of economic growth in the Philippines and in Vietnam

	Philippines		Vietnam	
Economic activity	% of GDP growth 2005–2019	CAGR 2005-2019	% of GDP growth 2005–2019	CAGR 2005–2019
Wholesale and retail trade; repair of motor vehicles and motorcycles	19.0	9.2	8.2	4.4
Manufacturing	15.9	6.3	21.6	7.3
Financial and insurance activities	9.8	11.0	6.6	7.2
Construction	9.1	12.1	7.1	6.8
Professional and business services	7.8	14.3	1.7	5.6
Agriculture, forestry, and fishing	6.8	5.2	7.8	2.7
Real estate and ownership of dwellings	6.6	8.4	3.3	3.5

Note the 'Professional and business services' category is not an account in Vietnam. 'Administrative and support service activities' and 'professional, scientific and technical activities' are used as a substitute and together contributed 1.7% of GDP growth. ***Data sources*** GSO Vietnam 2021, Philippine Statistics Authority 2021

regarding international trade and financing as well as partial equitization (equivalent to privatisation outside of Vietnam) from 1986 onwards meant that the economy opened up from 1994. The result was rapid economic growth.

It might be argued that the choice of calendar years and not policy explains the rate of growth. After all, the rate of growth of Vietnam was worse than that of the Philippines from 1960 to 1990 and the rate of growth of the Philippines from 1994 to 2019 was similar to that of Vietnam. External and internal fact checks belie this argument. Most other countries in Southeast Asia and most other countries in the world grew more quickly than the Philippines in the second half of the twentieth century. The stagnation of the Philippines was internally caused and not characteristic of the time period. The Philippines were at peace and independent from 1960 to 1992, while Vietnam was at war and then under embargo during that same period.

Examination and comparison of the two countries from 1994 to 2019 is also instructive. Each country has opened to a partial extent and has achieved impressive GDP growth (see Fig. 4.1 Recent economic growth of The Philippines and Vietnam), albeit with Vietnam outpacing the Philippines. However, closer examination reveals contrasting stories and results.

Most of the Philippine GDP growth is in services, especially retailing (contributing 18% of GDP in 2019) and business process outsourcing (about 7% of 2019 GDP, this category is not separate in national accounts). The business process outsourcing category truly brings some new money in the country, creating low to mid-skill jobs for a large number of people. Allowing foreign direct investment into this industry

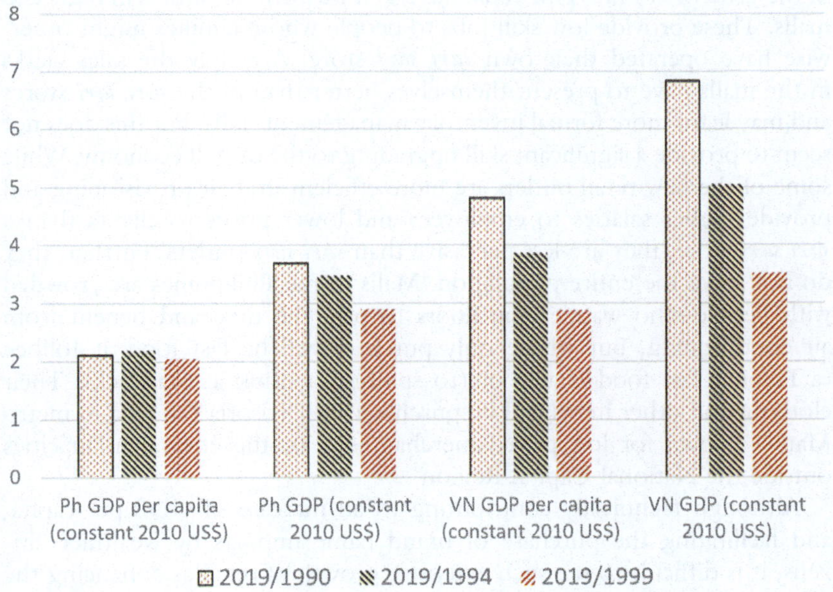

Fig. 4.1 Recent economic growth of The Philippines and Vietnam (*Data sources* World Bank national accounts data, OECD National Accounts data files and United Nations Population Division. World Population Prospects: 2019 Revision, Census reports and other statistical publications from national statistical offices, and United Nations Statistical Division, Population and Vital Statistics Report [various years])

did not threaten the business interests of the established elite families as, worldwide, the industry only emerged around 1990. Allowing foreign investment brought in the new retail players who did not represent competition to established families, although they are perhaps partial threats to the *sari sari* stores to be found through neighbourhoods of the lower economic levels of 75% of the population. They are above all new clients for the real estate developers, again belonging to the established elite. The retail industry contributes to the economy—in theory—by rendering the distribution of products more efficient. How large should the retail sector be? Publicly available data groups retail and wholesale with repair of motor vehicles and motorcycles. The average size for most countries is around for this category of businesses about 10% of GDP, contrasting dramatically with the 18% of the Philippines. Further, much of the growth of Philippine retail has taken the form of outlets in high-end malls. These provide low skill jobs to people whose families might otherwise have operated their own *sari sari* store. Arguably the sales clerks in the malls have to present themselves better than in the *sari sari* stores and may learn more formal inventory management skills, but this does not seem to provide a significant skill upgrading to the overall economy. While some of the new retail outlets are more efficient in their provisioning and provide higher salaries to employees and lower prices to clients than a *sari sari* store, they are less pervasive than *sari sari* outlets. Further, they do not serve the entire population. Malls in the Philippines are crowded with people who wander the floors to pass the time and benefit from air conditioning, but whose only purchase will be fast food at Jolibee (a Filipino fast food chain) or (to splurge) a drink at Starbucks. Their clothing and other items will be purchased in Divisoria (an area in metro Manila known for low-priced merchandise), or the equivalent in cities outside the National Capital Region.

Although technically contributing to an increase of GDP per capita, and facilitating the purchase of brand name imports by wealthier citizens, it is difficult to see such extensive growth of retail as enhancing the Philippine capacity to generate wealth rather than revealing the capacity to acquire goods and services. Since remittances increase household incomes by over a third, perhaps much of the increase of GDP is being generated cash coming from outside the country.

In contrast to the retail trade, a significant (30%) portion of the value added in business process outsourcing is exported, roughly the exports/GDP ratio for the overall economy, with virtually all domestically generated (compared with 77% for the overall economy). Again though, for a large number of jobs in this industry, the main skill acquired is 'international' English.

Manufacturing did contribute almost 16% of economic growth from 2005 to 2019, but it is growing more slowly than most services, and barely more quickly than agriculture.

Four activities contributed 63% of the increase of GDP in Vietnam over the years 2005–2019.[2] Wholesale, retail and vehicle repair is one of these activities, contributing 8.2% of growth, and in 2019 constituted 9.9% of GDP, about average for most economies. Manufacturing is far more important for the growth of Vietnam and contributed 26% of growth, even if this domestic generation of value is only half of the value of exports from manufacture (the other half being imported materials and parts). It represented 19.1% of GDP in 2019. Agriculture, forestry and fisheries contributed 7.8% of GDP growth and represented 13.7% of 2019 GDP. The fourth activity, construction, accounted for 7.1% of the increase of GDP from 2005 to 2019 and 6.6% of 2019 GDP. (All statistics calculated from data at GSO [2021])

This comparison of the Philippines and Vietnam over the past 25–20 years suggests that Vietnam has opened up more than the Philippines, and has benefitted more because of this aperture. On the other hand, foreign investment into Philippine business process outsourcing has been beneficial. Part of that success is due to widespread knowledge of English, and also no doubt because of the long-suffering character of most Filipinos, ideal for dealing with irate customers.

Rodrik's work (2015) showed that much manufacturing moved not from rich countries but from Latin America to East Asia. It is not correct to conclude that globalisation necessarily leads to premature de-industrialisation. Rather, it has caused this in some countries (some Latin American countries, for example), but not all. Vietnam, open to the influences of globalisation, is not suffering from premature deindustrialisation, while the Philippines, more isolated from global economic influences, indeed seems to be deindustrialising.

FDI flow into Vietnam has been far more significant and has led to a high trade (exports +imports) to GDP: ratio, but this FDI-financed trade is merchandise: oriented and generates modest domestic value added in exports.

Openness to financing and international trade clearly can bring benefits in the form of increased prosperity in line with a thesis of the first chapter:

use foreign capital to increase domestic productivity, and sell produce abroad to bring additional capital into the country. However, the cases also show that the terms and 'quality' of FDI projects affect just how advantageous than openness can be.[3]

Colonial exploitation would be an example of low quality 'FDI'. Most colonies did benefit somewhat by improved infrastructure and access to some medicines; however, while the objectives and competence of colonial administrations may often have brought some improvements, they rarely resulted in great prosperity for the colonies or the indigenous people in those colonies, while the colonisers usually benefitted greatly, either personally or as a nation. This was not only a problem of political and cultural subjugation, but also one of poor terms of the FDI 'deals' and an aperture to trade that carried implicitly regressive industrial policies.

Two Conjectures About Autarky

Can any nation or even any group of nations go it alone? While autarky or economic isolation is an impractical proposition, international trade has been raised as a bogeyman for national prosperity by more than one politician across the globe. It is obvious that Singapore, Hong Kong, Switzerland or Denmark would suffer if isolated from world trade and world capital. None of these countries could hope to either finance or populate factories of a reasonably economic scale to produce the variety of goods they currently enjoy, even if services are excluded from our consideration. International trade is more advantageous to firms in smaller countries (Shachmurove and Spiegel 2004). It could be argued that this problem of size that could be overcome by the largest countries on the planet. The three largest in population are India (18% of the world population), China (18%) and the United States of America (4%). The following paragraphs carry out two rather speculative and naïve conjectures about a large nation isolating itself in order to help clarify the impracticality of the pursuit of prosperity through autarky. The first conjecture is an autarkic economic unit based on demographic size: can China go for it alone? The second conjecture is an autarkic economic unit based on current economic size: can the United States of America go for it alone? These conjectures will focus upon trade alone and omit considerations of international finance.

Autarky for a very large-sized population Asia has the 58% of the world population. However, if we divide up the world into blocs of countries with some sort of common ground, we quickly discard Asia as a group because of geographic extension and myriad disparities. Even if we were to use such a physical criterion as skin colour, it makes as much sense to include the entire Eurasian and Africa land mass. Table 4.4 presents one way to divide up the planet.

Among all these blocs, only China and India are distinct political entities. The government of China is far more independent of the influence of interest groups, although there may be debate about stability. India politics seems characterised longer term trends in party dominance; however, power is maintained by a combination of reinforcing the elites and simplistic ideology for the masses. The result is a less consistently directive government. Bloc 5 could potentially get its act together for some form of economic unity if it can overcome tensions between Japan and Korea as well as the geo-political issue of Taiwan's sovereignty that has been swept under the carpet for a few decades.

Realistically and in the short term, China is the only 'bloc' that could have a shot at autarky based on the size of population and the ability of its administration to act.

More than four decades of concerted effort by China's government to prioritise economic growth has been based on partially opening up the economy: exploiting an epoch of cheap and dexterous labour to become world assembler, and then enticing firms from wealthy countries with

Table 4.4 Blocs of the world by population

	Bloc	*Population*	*% world population*
1	Americas and Europe	1.71	22
2	China	1.39	18
3	India	1.35	17
4	Sub-Saharan Africa	1.10	14
5	Japan, Korea, Taiwan, ASEAN, Bangladesh, Sri Lanka and Oceania	1.08	14
6	North Africa and Middle East	0.58	7
7	Countries with more than 50% identified Islam	1.4	18
	Total 1–6	7	92

Data source author's calculations from publicly available data deriving from national census results

its immense market and acquiring technical and management knowledge from them with varying degrees of aggression, and finally establishing itself as world class manufacturer in various industries. Language seems to limit China's success at exporting services, but manufacturing cannot succeed independently of services, so at least some of these must also be at a world class level.

Can China now find an autarkic economy upon this success? There are several obstacles that seem difficult to overcome, as analysis of imports and export indicates.

Imports The Atlas of Economic Complexity lists 4,565 categories of imports by China. The sheer number of import categories (not individual products, but categories of products) already contains an important piece of information: there are 300,000 Chinese for each category, or 164,355 Chinese participating in the labour force available for each category—if everyone worked in agriculture, extraction, utilities and manufacture. Since 42.3% of the labour force is employed in services, we are left about 86,000 persons. However, not all categories of products are imported. There are about 8500 different categories in the Harmonised Commodity Description and Coding System. Assuming that the Chinese economy would require the majority of these, we are down to about 40,000 in the labour force available for each category of imports. Many factories produce a variety of products, but fewer produce a variety of categories of products. Nonetheless, it would seem that China has sufficient labour force to produce this variety of products and workers for factories substituting for imports. Foxconn's two largest factories in (Longhua and Zhengzhou) each several hundred thousand employees, but such behemoths are counterbalanced by the more numerous smaller factories.

Since this is a simple thought experiment, only the largest 20 import categories are examined here (see Table 4.5). At first glance, the table suggests that, after an adjustment period during which the government administration would have to combine a judicious mix of direct management with market incentives to cultivate various industries, it would be possible for China to attain an autarky substituting for all imports.

Of course, if we were to ask the opinion of business persons in any somewhat sophisticated industry, there would be certainly be protests that there is so much detail being overlooked. Integrated circuits may be one category, but many kinds of factories are involved, each with its peculiar design, fabrication, testing and packaging challenges. A similar

Table 4.5 Major imports to China and potential for import substitution

HS6 classification	*Trade Value (million $US)*	*% TOTAL IMPORTS*	*Resource, Intermediate or Final product*	*Comments*
Petroleum oils, oils from bituminous minerals, crude	207,603	12.9	R	Most natural resource reserves can be increased by intensive exploration. See Gelb et al. (2012)
Monolithic integrated circuits, digital	130,318	8.1	I	China does have a domestic industry, including design, fabrication, packaging and testing. Huawei overtook Qualcomm as SOC supplier to China manufactured smartphones in 2020 (in part by necessity)
Iron ore, concentrate, not iron pyrites, unagglomerated	55,777	3.5	R	
Soya beans	33,797	2.1	F	
Copper ores and concentrates	31,677	2.0	R	China is the third-largest producer worldwide but still imports 80% of consumption. It has begun stockpiling copper (Desai 2020)

(continued)

Table 4.5 (continued)

HS6 classification	*Trade Value (million $US)*	*% TOTAL IMPORTS*	*Resource, Intermediate or Final product*	*Comments*
Medium-Sized Cars	31,280	1.9	F	China has a robust automobile manufacturing industry
Gold in unwrought forms non-monetary	28,560	1.8	R	
Fixed wing aircraft, unladen weight > 15,000 kg	27,629	1.7	F	China has a weak incipient airplane manufacture industry, including airliners
Oils petroleum, bituminous, distillates, except crude	27,199	1.7	R	
Natural gas, liquefied	23,208	1.4	R	
Parts of line telephone/telegraph equipment, not elsewhere specified	22,952	1.4	I	China does have a domestic industry
Copper cathodes and sections of cathodes unwrought	22,383	1.4	I	Domestic manufacture limited by reserves
Machines and mechanical appliances, not elsewhere specified	21,440	1.3	F	This is a wide catch-all category
Parts and accessories of data processing equipment, not elsewhere specified	18,165	1.1	I	This is a wide catch-all category
Optical devices, appliances and instruments, not elsewhere specified	16,851	1.0	F	This is a wide catch-all category

(continued)

Table 4.5 (continued)

HS6 classification	*Trade Value (million $US)*	*% TOTAL IMPORTS*	*Resource, Intermediate or Final product*	*Comments*
P-xylene	16,222	1.0	F	China does have a chemical industry
Bituminous coal, not agglomerated	16,183	1.0	R	
Transmissions for motor vehicles	13,282	0.8	I	China does manufacture transmissions
Parts for radio/tv transmit/receive equipment, not elsewhere specified	12,670	0.8	I	China does manufacture radio parts
Medicaments, not elsewhere specified, in dosage	11,199	0.7	F	

Data sources Desai (2020), Litho World (2020), and Gelb et al. (2012); Made in China website; various industry analyses

comment can be may for 'medicaments' and for the 'not elsewhere specified' catch-all categories. Even reasonably well-defined categories such as transmissions for motor vehicles imply multiple product-market groups with multiple competitors. For most of the more complex production, China would have to up the ante for acquiring foreign intellectual property by whatever means possible to avoid falling far behind. Finally, a third of the top imports are natural resources. The search for additional reserves of natural resources withing national boundaries will eventually lead to finds, but often to more costly sources of ores, less fertile land, etc. (see Gelb et al. [2012] and Adelman and Watkins [2008] to delve a little deeper into resource costs).

Complete import substitution might be conceivable, but the current administration wisely pursues a different path, gradually substituting and surpassing selected technologies, using external competition to help select winners (not only domestic rivals as did Korea's Park Chung-hee).

Examination of any of the problematic import or export categories in greater detail would probably raise more issues, but this superficial consideration of trade suppression suggests higher costs would be the first consequence of isolation. Even if innovation could be reinforced with industrial espionage and other techniques to steal intellectual property, the incentives to implement technical progress will be diminished by the reduction of domestic rivalry (and of the number of domestic rivals for some formerly exporting industries). The variety of consumer goods would be reduced. Besides all of these evident implications, there is the real challenge of implementing this isolation with the economic changes required by it. It is a massive practical problem, probably best solved by the market as constraints are introduced by government.

Exports China exported US$2.59 trillion of goods in 2018. This compares with the GDP figure of 13.6 trillion. Agriculture, hunting, forestry, fishing (7%) and mining, manufacturing (also reported as a separate subgroup), construction, electricity, water and gas (39%) together total 46% of GDP (World Bank national accounts data, and OECD National Accounts data files). Although the utilities contribute little to international trade, this total—about US$6.26 trillion—provides a rough estimate of the tradeable goods production of China's economy. This means that about 40% of China's production is exported. In turn, this implies that autarky would impose a decrease in the number of rival firms with greater than the minimum economic scale of production (the minimum to benefit from economies of scale; this changes as technology and machinery changes). This is immaterial in many industries that are fragmented, but may bring consequences in industries with more complex processes or short product cycles. Table 4.6 lists and comments the top ten categories of merchandise exported by China; as only the top eight exports account for more than 1% of total exports, the table is abbreviated compared to Table 4.5 (Major imports to China).

Three categories of exports pose the problem of minimum scale of production: Transmit-receive apparatus for radio and TV, Monolithic integrated circuits, computer CPUs with some of storage/input/output. The petroleum category raises the issue of the complexity of this industry and downstream processing, all scale sensitive and most needing reliable feedstock. Depriving domestic producers of world markets would severely impact domestic industry structures and at minimum lead to higher costs and prices, and probably reduced variety for end consumers.

This admittedly brief and superficial examination of current international trade by Chinese businesses—both imports and exports—suggests that isolating the economy of China would inevitably leads to higher costs

Table 4.6 Top ten exports by China

HS6	*Trade value $US billion*	*% total exports*	*Comment*
Transmit-receive apparatus for radio, TV, etc.	223,442	8.6	Scale is probably an issue for many products as these are not mass-market items
Computer data storage units	105,194	4.1	Scale is an issue, but China possibly has a large enough market
Parts and accessories of data processing equipment, not elsewhere specified	98,878	3.8	Scale is an issue, but China possibly has a large enough market
Monolithic integrated circuits, digital	89,102	3.4	Scale and short life cycle are issues
Parts of line telephone/telegraph equipment, not elsewhere specified	52,824	2.0	The world market is dominated by 5 firms. This is partly due to ease of fit of diverse components of the same brand, but scale is also a factor. However, China does have about 1/5 of the world population
Oils petroleum, bituminous, distillates, except crude	31,216	1.2	While China would need to retain all petroleum production while increasing known reserves, this raises the issue of the complexity of the petroleum industry
Toys, not elsewhere specified	29,578	1.1	This is not a crucial industry

(continued)

Table 4.6 (continued)

HS6	*Trade value $US billion*	*% total exports*	*Comment*
Colour television receivers/monitors/projectors	27,179	1.1	Three of the largest eight television manufacturers worldwide are located in China, but over 40% of the world market is controlled by Japan and Korea. There are about 50 each of LCD and OLED display fabrication plants worldwide
Digital computer CPU with some of storage/input/output	22,214	0.9	Scale and short life cycle are issues
Static converters, not elsewhere specified	20,214	0.8	There is a relatively large number of firms worldwide

Data sources AEC (2020) and author's calculations

and prices, and probably lead to reduced technical progress even under conditions of free access to foreign intellectual property

Autarky for a very large economy The media give the impression that the United States of America and China are neck-and-neck in terms of economic clout. Although China has been growing quickly, it is still in a different class from the US both in terms of brute economic volume and in terms of the level of material wealth of its citizens (as indicated, for example, by GDP per capita). Demographic trends are also beginning to constrain economic potential. Table 4.7 lists and groups the largest nations by GDP. The following paragraphs discuss the viability of isolating the economy of the United States.

A variety of opinions and interests influence American actions and policies, although these almost always give priority to domestic prosperity in the short to mid-term. The current and previous administrations have not embraced a crass isolationism, but there is a distinct concern with the dangers of depending upon 'critical' production outside of its United States as well as complaints about American CEOs creating jobs abroad

Table 4.7 Largest nations by GDP

Nations	*2019 GDP in current trillion $US*
US	21
China	14
Japan and Germany	5 & 4
India, UK, France	a little under 3
Italy, Brazil, Canada, Russia, and South Korea	2
Australia, Spain and Mexico	from 1.3 to 1.4
Indonesia and the Netherlands	around 1 trillion

Data source Author's calculations from World Bank national accounts data, and OECD National Accounts data files

while abandoning their fellow citizens (see endnote 1 for recent research on the impact of imports from China on jobs). The Covid-19 pandemic highlighted the supposed security issue for items such as surgical and N-95 masks and personal protective equipment. Still, microprocessor production dominance by Taiwan, fear of competition for Boeing and Brazil, China, Russia and Vietnam's possessing 83% of known rare earth reserves are just some of the indicators that the United States of America cannot prosper in isolation.

Microprocessor fabrication (distinct from design) requires massive scale and will continue to do so until successive generations bring little technical improvement and clients realise this. Even control of 24% of world demand (via a greater percentage of the market for premium electronic gadgets) would leave the country at a handicap with respect to fabricators for the other 76%. The microprocessor industry is especially illustrative. The designs of 2021 can be produced only after the experience of production and design of previous generations. Even a team of geniuses with a fleet of twenty-first century computers would have been unable to imagine the 2021 design and production process and equipment in 1970 without the 50 years of experience accumulated since that time. That experience was incredibly expensive, financed predominantly by revenues from an ever-growing market. Isolating microprocessors from the world market would have been feasible only at the cost of either slowing down experience (producing less per unit of time), or else by a financial regime that funnelled national resources into that industry at the cost of others, in the same way that the USSR sacrificed its economy as a whole for the development of space research and the armed forces until its economy came close to foundering.

U.S. fear of competition for Boeing (manifested, for example, in the flubbed treatment of Bombardier's C-series and in regulatory failures regarding the 737 Max) is well-founded for similar reasons. The world airliner market is effectively a duopoly, with competition from Japan, China and Russia far behind Airbus and Boeing. A change in the structure of the market would be very painful for either player, yet the manufacture of airliners is important for the transport of goods and people across the country and abroad. Restricting the market of Boeing to the United States would slow the development of innovative design and manufacture that meet safety standards of the same reason: scale would be reduced and experience would become far more expensive either in time or in appropriation of national resources.

The United States of America is a large country with abundant natural resources, and also a voracious appetite for those resources. Rare earths (elements 21, 39 and 57–71 on the periodic table) are one important example. Rare earths are used as catalysts and as phosphors (materials that luminesce), and some oxides are used to polish glass. They are critical ingredients in most electronic devices, both consumer and military. However, mining, refining and disposal of rare earths pose serious environmental problems (Terrascope 2016) so that, like plastic recycling, most prospecting and assaying has been done in countries with less stringent environmental constraints. The result is that Brazil, China, Russia and Vietnam possess 83% of known rare earth reserves. In 2019, China (57%), the U.S.A. (16%) and Burma/Myanmar (12%) accounted for 85% of world production. Autarky would confront the USA with the choice between accepting the pollution or of decreasing its dependence on electronic devices. Unfortunately, the minimalist philosophy applies poorly to electronic devices for a reason alluded to earlier: technical progress depends upon expensive practical experience as much as it does upon theoretical research. Quality is not accessible without quantity. Pollution would be the short-term choice, with the hope of discovering less polluting processes.

It follows that perhaps countries with a very large economy like the United States of America could 'go it' alone, but only by sacrificing their prosperity and quality of life relative to the rest of the world.

The Reality of International Trade

Autarky is not a practical project. Historical failures from Ming China through Sakoku Japan to Hoxha's Albania suggest that autarky only occurs when governments are willing to sacrifice economic prosperity to reinforce control. A more realistic approach—although not the ideal for world prosperity—is a controlled approach to trade with a judiciously permeable border. Governments respond to both to pressure from interest groups and economic opportunity in implementing rules that control cross-border transactions. The example of the Philippines illustrates the dangers of weak governments that are over-responsive to domestic interests. History—Germany in the decades following 1879, much of United States of America history before World War II, Japan from World War II until the 1980s, and Korea from 1962 to the mid-1990s—suggests that strong governments managing the volume and nature cross border transactions is advantageous for individual countries if not for the global economy (Studwell 2014). Arguably, the entire world has benefitted from the successes of the U.S., Germany, Japan and Korea.

General openness is advantageous, as argued by Smith and Ricardo, but completely uncontrolled international trade and investment would lead to the relative stagnation of poorer countries if domestic firms cannot compete and if foreign investment extracts all value while using domestic resources. Governments moderate the openness of national economies. This pragmatic approach to trade and foreign investment is what really characterises international agreements, in spite of official discourse about the benefits of an open world economy.

Foreign investors enter into transactions with local parties, but do so within ground rules set by the host government. The government of any host country should establish solid terms for foreign direct investments.[4] However, the ability of the host government to establish terms for foreign investment is in turn often constrained by ground rules set by trade agreements with the government of the home nation.[5]

Some national leaders have been able to convince their electorate of the advantages of withdrawal from free trade agreements of various sorts, or of protecting local industry. The United States of America has been withdrawing from the world for the last decade, notably from world trade and the governance of international institutions—although this withdrawal can be exaggerated in the media, as Professor Shambaugh (2021) has recently observed. The United Kingdom withdrew from the European Union on February 1 2020, although the provocative issue was sovereignty rather than free trade. Narendra Modi, the current prime minister of India, has encourage the electorate to buy local to promote a self-sufficient India (*aatmanirbhar Bharat*)—although his finance minister was quick to explain that this was not isolationism.

Part of the motivation may be that world leaders are politicians whose thirst for power may eclipse their desire to serve their country, and seek hot issues that will garner votes. However, it is also true that there is little historical experience of true openness. Trade agreements are not always between equal parties. China has often been accused of bullying other countries, but neither the EU nor the United States of America have feared 'realpolitik' as a euphemism for 'might makes right'. Although individual citizens of any country may be noble-hearted and seek the good of humanity rather than their own, the people who forge free trade agreements believe more in process than principle—often once again letting might make right. The result is not free trade, but complicated terms of trade.

This is the deeper practical reason that makes the advantages of free trade and capital elusive: there is no such thing as a free trade agreement.

A true free trade agreement would be 3–4 pages long. It would state that are to be no tariffs nor non-tariff measures between the parties effective at a given date. It would stipulate a duration, renewal date and process for renewal. It would also detail a procedure for policing the agreement and penalties for transgressions. The North American Free Trade Agreement was somewhat longer... at about 1700 pages. The agreement which replaced it—the Agreement between the United States of America, the United Mexican States, and Canada—has 34 chapters, 4 annexes (or 13, depending how you count them) and 16 side letters varying from 1 to 5 pages long.

Why are free trade agreements so long? There are two reasons.

The first is that trade is not free according to these agreements. There are exceptions and stipulations. All imports entering the USA from Canada or Mexico are duty free ... if the value is below $US117. All imports entering the USA from Canada or Mexico are tax free... if the value is below US$50 (entering from Mexico) or if the value is below US$40 (entering from Canada). Trade between the two countries is still subject to barriers. In addition, the trade agreement is phrased to limit trade with the rest of the world. For example, automobiles can be imported into the United States of America tariff-free on the following conditions:

- 40–45% of auto content be made by workers earning at least $16 per hour;
- 75% of auto content be made in North America;
- 70% of a vehicle's steel and aluminium must originate in North America, steel must be melted and poured in region.

Again, if any of the parties were to enter into a trade agreement with a non-market economy (as interpreted by the administration of each country; under the Trump administration—and probably the current Biden administration—this meant China), then the other parties would no longer be bound by the agreement.

The second reason that free trade agreements are so long is implementation: it is not an easy task to make trade truly free. For example, it is reasonable that governments protect their citizens from unnecessary danger. It can be complicated, however, for two or more different governments to have exactly the same rules to protect their citizens. When two trading countries do not have identical rules, goods and services coming into each country must be screened for conformity, resulting in unintentional non-tariff trade barriers. The same applies to other rules besides the immediate safety of citizens, such as child labour rules, environment protection, etc. The only way to achieve frictionless mobility of goods and services is to impose the same rules upon all parties, and this implies a legislator with the authority to impose such rules and agencies to police them. This in turn leads to resentment of impaired sovereignty such as inspired the Brexit movement.

Ideological movements, whether or not well-founded, also generate obstacles to international trade. For example, the climate change movement would require central African and Amazonian countries to limit deforestation, although most of the activists (although far from all) hail from countries that are wealthy today thanks to centuries eliminating their own forests (mostly recovered in the twenty-first century). Thus, 'sustainability' becomes a requirement of any trade agreement with poorer countries. Again, politicians may seize upon these concerns of the public to mask protectionist measures.

Although all this seems to make the waters murky, it becomes clear that the insights of Smith and Ricardo should be understood intelligently and not simplistically. International trade can benefit all, but many other factors influence the prosperity of a nation, so that theoretical models and empirical tests will return mixed results depending on how they are engineered. Similarly, FDI can be very beneficial, but many factors simultaneously influence the prosperity of a nation. The real question is not if trade and FDI are beneficial, but how to ensure that the nation benefits rather than squander opportunities.

Frederick List acknowledged the advantage of free trade in an ideal world, but considered it folly to embrace 'the system of Adam Smith in its present imperfection, leave their national interests to the direction of foreign nations and foreign laws, because in a more perfect but entirely imaginary state of the human race, free trade would be beneficial to mankind'. (List 1827, Letter 1). Smith, Ricardo and List himself lived in a far simpler world than ours. It is possible that Smith and Ricardo intended their assertions to be applied simplistically in that simple world as List has interpreted Smith. However, it is far more fertile to improve our understanding of how economies work than to debate the intention of eighteenth and nineteenth century thinkers. Then political leaders, technocrats, researchers and others can work towards a world where international trade, investment and even labour are freer to cross borders than they are today.

Notes

1. 'We will: champion open economies and societies; promote global economic resilience; harness the digital economy with data free flow with trust'.—G7 leaders' statement, February 19, 2021 (European Council 2021). A separate question is whether the outflow of capital from the home country to the host country is beneficial to the host country. Current demagoguery is that it is obviously detrimental because it creates jobs in foreign countries instead of jobs at home. However, businesses invest, not countries, and businesses invest to the benefit of the overall business, suggesting that the freedom to invest abroad is important for any large firm and thus to maintain existing jobs. Autor et al. (2013) provide a high-profile research article arguing for jobs in the U.S.A. being lost to imports from China, and with data for replication provided (Autor et al. 2019).

However, Magyari (2017) arrives at opposing results by considering expansion of affected firms into areas of competitive advantage, Rothwell (2017) found domestic shocks are equal or greater factors in job loss than imports from China and that unemployment risk in non-traded sectors is at least as high as in traded sectors. Kiyota and co-authors (2021) examine the effects of imports from China on employment in six advanced countries: France, Germany, Japan, South Korea, the United Kingdom and the United States, distinguishing between imports of final goods and those of intermediate inputs. The positive effects of the latter 'offset or even outweigh' the negative effects of the former.

2. At the time of writing, 2019 data were preliminary.
3. 'Historically, the quality of investment has been at least as important for growth as the quantity. Although the fastest growing countries had higher rates of investment than the others in Table 2.1 [of the World bank report], empirical studies generally find that less than half the growth in output is attributable to increases in labour and capital. Higher productivity explains the rest. Higher labour productivity reflects better health, skills, education, and work effort; higher capital productivity reflects technical progress and the more efficient use of saving' (World Bank 1989, pp. 29–30). This notion of quality of FDI appeared sporadically in various publications of post-World War II international economic institutions, but did not appear in the academic research literature until Alfaro and Charlton (2013), as distinct from quality of investment flows, quality of investment institutions, investment climate, investment promotion, investment protection and perhaps other differing topics. Since then, the OECD has begun to champion the notion of 'indicators' of quality FDI, grouped into five clusters—productivity and innovation, employment and job quality, skills, gender equality and the carbon footprint. (OECD 2019, pp. 4 and 12). While the first three clusters are relevant to the concerns of this book (and I believe, of most developing countries), the other clusters are either only indirectly relevant and in the mid to long term, laudable though they may be in absolute terms. The actual indicators are difficult to recognize both in the OECD document (2019) and in its predecessor (Lejárraga and Ragoussis 2018): they are existent statistics available from the World Bank and other organisations and compiled from surveys and national accounts. Some desirable outcomes of FDI

for our proposed objective of prosperity are: higher labour productivity, R&D intensity, creation of secure jobs with good wages, skill intensity, on-the-job training.

4. What are 'solid terms' for foreign direct investment? A reasonable part of the value generated by the investment should remain in the host country in the form of wages, taxes, positive secondary effects such as knowledge, an increase in domestic supplier industries without undue negative side effects such as pollution, exhaustion of natural resources.
5. Adam Smith, for example, showed how the dynamics of price equilibria in four markets (land, capital, labour and product) could divert capital to the production most desired by citizens; but in the same book he warns that 'we' must beware producers conniving to fix prices. This might be interpreted as the need to protect the free market, but it is also a dose of realism: price can do a pretty good job at distributing goods and services, but it is not perfect nor immune to human manipulation. In spite of this many writers of the past two centuries have purported selfishness to be the basis of prosperity and even of democracy and the justice system, with process being more important than good will for the pursuit of the common good. Bew (2019) has documented how the notion of real politik has undergone a somewhat similar distortion from realistically dealing with circumstances as they are while working towards a better world, to cynical pursuit of own's national interest because, well, everybody else is doing it.

References

Adelman, M.A., and G.C. Watkins. 2008. Reserve Prices and Mineral Resource Theory. *The Energy Journal* 29: 1–16.

AEC. 2020. Atlas of Economic Complexity. https://atlas.cid.harvard.edu/. Accessed November 5, 2021.

Alfaro, Laura, and Andrew Charlton. 2013. Growth and the Quality of Foreign Direct Investment: Is All FDI Equal? In *The Industrial Policy Revolution I: The Role of Government Beyond Ideology*, no. 151–1, ed. Joseph E. Stiglitz and Justin Lin Yifu. IEA Conference Volume. London: Palgrave Macmillan.

Autor, David H., David Dorn, and Gordon H. Hanson. 2013. The China Syndrome: Local Labor Market Effects of Import Competition in the United States. *The American Economic Review* 103 (6): 2121–2168.

Autor, David H., David Dorn, and Gordon H. Hanson. 2019. Replication Data for: The China Syndrome: Local Labor Market Effects of Import Competition in the United States. OpenICPSR. Available at https://www.openicpsr.org/openicpsr/project/112670/version/V1/view;jsessionid=E4D8537C9250F0DC98E8EB15092597A0. Accessed March 15, 2021.

Bew, John. 2019. *Real Politik. A History*. Oxford: Oxford University Press.

Desai, Pratima. 2020. China's Blueprint to Stockpile Copper in 5-year Plan. *Reuters*. Available at https://www.reuters.com/article/china-copper-stockpiles/graphic-chinas-blueprint-to-stockpile-copper-expected-in-5-year-plan-idINL8N2HA5MF. Accessed February 24, 2021

European Council 2021. G7 Leaders' Statement. February 19, https://www.consilium.europa.eu/en/press/press-releases/2021/02/19/g7-february-leaders-statement/. Accessed February 23, 2021.

Gelb, Alan, Kai Kaiser, and Lorena Viñuela. 2012. How Much Does Natural Resource Extraction Really Diminish National Wealth? The Implications of Discovery. Center for Global Development. Working Paper 290

GSO. 2021. National Accounts. Available at https://www.gso.gov.vn/en/px-web/?pxid=E0306-07&theme=National%20Accounts%20and%20State%20budget. Accessed February 4, 2020.

Kiyota, Kozo, Sawako Maruyama, and Mina Taniguchi. 2021. The China Syndrome: A Cross-Country Evidence. University Keio-IES Discussion Paper Series Institute for Economic Studies, Keio. Available at https://ies.keio.ac.jp/en/publications/13671/. Accessed March 15, 2021. Two different sequences of authors priority are given.

Lejárraga, Iza, and Alexandros Ragoussis. 2018. Beyond Capital. Monitoring Development Outcomes of Multinational Enterprise. International Finance Corporation (World Bank Group). Available at http://documents1.worldbank.org/curated/en/342571545336579695/pdf/WPS8686.pdf. Accessed December 12, 2020.

List, Frederick. 1827. Outlines of American Political Economy in a Series of Letters Addressed by Frederic List, Esq. Late Professor of Political Economy at the University of Tubingen to Charles J Ingersoll, Esq. Samuel Parker, Philadelphia.

Litho World. 2020. Recent Progress of the Integrated Circuit Industry in China — Overview of the Manufacturing Industry. Available at http://lithotechsolutions.com/p/58/. Accessed February 24, 2021.

Magyari, Ildikó. 2017. Firm Reorganization, Chinese Imports, and US Manufacturing Employment. Availble at https://econpapers.repec.org/paper/cenwpaper/17-58.htm. Accessed March 15, 2021.

Minh, Cao Hong. 2020. Remittances, Foreign Direct Investment, Imports and Economic Growth: Empirical Evidence from Vietnam. *Asian Journal of Economic Modelling* 8 (2): 133–140.

Nguyen, Phuc Hien. 2017. Remittances and Competitiveness: A Case Study of Vietnam. *Journal of Economics, Business and Management* 5 (2): 79–83.

OECD. 2019. FDI Qualities Indicators. Measuring the sustainable development impacts of investment. Available at PSA. 2021. National Accounts of the Philippines as of January 2021. Philippine Statistics Authority.

Rodrik, Dani. 2015. Premature Deindustrialization. *Journal of Economic Growth* 21: 1–33.

Rothwell, Jonathan. 2017. Cutting the Losses: Reassessing the Costs of Import Competition to Workers and Communities. Available at SSRN https://ssrn.com/abstract=2920188. Accessed March 15, 2021.

Shachmurove, Yochanan, and Uriel Spiegel. 2004. Size Does Matter- International Trade and Population Size. PIER Working Paper 04-035.Penn Institute for Economic Research Available at https://economics.sas.upenn.edu/sites/default/files/filevault/working-papers/04-035.pdf.

Shambaugh, David. 2021. *Where Great Powers Meet: America and China in Southeast Asia*. Oxford: Oxford University Press.

Studwell, Joe. 2014. *How Asia Works*. Grove Press.

Terrascope. 2016. Mission 2016: Strategic Mineral Management. Available at https://web.mit.edu/12.000/www/m2016/finalwebsite/index.html. Accessed February 26, 2021.

Uniteller. 2019. Both Sides of the Coin. Remittances in Asia: Side One – The Receivers' Story. Avaialble at https://uniteller.com/the-receivers-story/. Accessed January 21, 2021.

Index

R. Macdonald, *Open and Closed Economies*,
https://doi.org/10.1007/978-3-030-79534-4

The manufacturer's authorised representative in the EU is Springer Nature Customer Service Centre GmbH, Europaplatz 3, 69115 Heidelberg, Germany. If you have any concerns regarding our products, please contact ProductSafety@springernature.com

Printed and bound by CPI Group (UK) Ltd, Croydon, CR0 4YY
30/09/2026
02225472-0009